A WINTER ON THE NILE,

IN EGYPT, AND IN NUBIA.

BY THE

REV. CHARLES D. BELL, D.D.,

Honorary Canon of Carlisle ; Rector of Cheltenham.

Author of " Gleanings from a Tour in Palestine and the East," " Night Scenes of the Bible," "Our Daily Life," etc., etc.

ISBN: 978-1-63923-624-4

Printed: January 2023

Published and Distributed By:
Lushena Books
607 Country Club Drive, Unit E
Bensenville, IL 60106
www.lushenabks.com

ISBN: 978-1-63923-624-4

DEDICATION.

TO MY

DEAR WIFE AND TWO DAUGHTERS,

IN MEMORY OF A DELIGHTFUL WINTER

PASSED TOGETHER IN EGYPT,

THIS VOLUME IS

AFFECTIONATELY DEDICATED.

PREFACE.

HAVING been recommended by a London physician to spend last winter in Egypt, I followed his advice, and found, from some months' residence in that delightful climate, the happiest results to my health, and a never-failing source of interest and pleasure. I had paid a brief visit to the country before ; but was glad, on this second occasion, to make a more prolonged stay.

There is no country but one so full of interest as Egypt, not only from its own wondrous history, but from its close connection with Bible story. I took copious notes, at the time, of what I saw, and heard, and read. Many are the books of deepest interest and instruction on this land ; and the following pages are a plain, unvarnished account of the impressions I received, and of the knowledge I gained.

The book is not intended for the Egyptologist, at

whose feet I would willingly sit as a learner, but for
the ordinary reader, to whom I would fain impart
something of the pleasure I received from " A Winter
on the Nile," and for the traveller who may be intend-
ing to visit the land of the Pharaohs. Egypt, like
Palestine, is a land of surpassing interest and undying
charm. The wonders of its old civilization ; of its
literature contained in religious books and scientific
treatises ; the marvels of its pyramids, its temples,
and its tombs, can never be exhausted ; the fascination increases with knowledge, and "increase of
appetite grows by what it feeds on." It may be said
of the country, as was said of its beautiful queen :—

> " Age cannot wither her, nor custom stale
>   Her infinite beauty ;
>   She makes hungry
>   Where most she satisfies."

In the course of the narrative I have made reference to many books and many writers ; and, in every
quotation, I have given the name of the author from
whose work the extract has been made.

It would be a pleasure to think that I had interested
any reader of my book so much as to induce him,
should it be in his power, to visit Egypt, and to see

for himself the charm of the Nile, the beauty of its table-lands and desert, and the ruins of temples and tombs which are still the wonder of the world.

Through the kindness of Dr. Thomas D. Saville, M.D., M.R.C.P., whose acquaintance I made in Egypt, I am able to add, at the end of the book, a series of careful meteorological observations on the changes of temperature on the Nile last winter—a fairly typical one, I believe—and which may be of some interest to the reader.

CONTENTS.

ix

CHAPTER I.

I T was delightful to exchange the fogs and rains
of England, the frosts and snows of Europe,
for the blue skies and clear atmosphere, the warmth
and sunshine of Egypt. And pleasant it was to
leave the restless and unquiet sea, and to find one's
self within the double harbour of Alexandria. The
steamer came to anchor there on the 29th of Decem-
ber, 1887 ; and one could hardly believe, as we
stepped on shore, in most brilliant weather, that it
was so near the close of the year. There was not
only sunshine, but many flowers were in bloom,—
the poinsettia, with its scarlet petals, which grows
to the size of a tall shrub ; the crimson hibiscus,
and the purple bougainvillea, whose rich deep purple
puts to shame the paler-hued blossom of our conser-
vatories.

B

before the eyes an ever-varying kaleidoscope of form and colour, and conjuring up memories of "The Arabian Nights."

Alexandria, the city of Alexander, even in its old days of splendour, was a comparatively modern city, being founded only 323 years before the Christian era, by the great conqueror who overran the world, and wept that there were no other worlds to conquer. It is modern when contrasted with Memphis, and Thebes, and Heliopolis—cities which date back to an age before history began. The present city is entirely modern, and only the name, and a few ruins, remain to recall the magnificent Alexandria which Strabo has described. Alexandria, which "claimed his peculiar protection," once "gloried," as Gibbon tells us, in the name of the "City of Serapis." Serapis was not originally an Egyptian deity—his worship was introduced there by Ptolemy Soter. As the population of Alexandria was composed of Greek and Egyptian elements, Ptolemy, to reconcile the two, introduced the Egyptian belief, under a Greek form. How was this to be done? He announced that he had been commanded by a dream to send for the god to Sinope on the Euxine, where he had been long worshipped ; and when his messengers returned with the sacred statue, they declared it to be Serapis, or Osiris, the husband of Isis, the celestial monarch of Egypt. Apis, the sacred bull worshipped at Memphis, was believed to be an incarnation of Osiris. The policy of Ptolemy was successful, and the worship of Osiris became general. A splendid temple was raised in his honour, where the god was worshipped for some time; but of the consecrated buildings, the stately halls, and exquisite statues, described by Gibbon, not a fragment remains. It was destroyed by the early Christians, whose indignation was excited by the honour paid to Serapis, and all sacrifices to the gods were abolished by the last edict of the Emperor Theodosius. Alexandria is a city of memories; its celebrated buildings are things of the past. The Pharos, the splendid lighthouse, one of the seven wonders of the world, built by Ptolemy Philadelphus, at a cost of £150,000 sterling, to light the way into the harbour, and which stood on a rock on the north-east extremity of the island of the same name, is gone, and has left no remains behind. The museum, founded by Ptolemy Soter, to which flocked the sages of ancient Greece, and which was long renowned as a school of science, philosophy, and literature, has disappeared, and even the exact site is doubtful. The famous library attached to the museum, which at the death of Ptolemy Philadelphus

the other to New York, to be placed amid un-
congenial surroundings. The obelisk which now
stands on the Thames Embankment was erected by
Thothmes III. of the 18th dynasty, who reigned
1,600 years B.C., and who inscribed this "needle"
with his own name. The Cæsareum, it is said, was
erected by Cleopatra to commemorate the birth of
her son by Julius Cæsar, and who was named
Cæsarion ; and the obelisk, which stood near the
temple of Cæsar, was called after the beautiful and
seductive queen. Would that these columns had
been left where they were, that the fallen one had
been raised on its old site, and that foreign energy
and liberality had found some other and more com-
mendable outflow.

Like other visitors to Alexandria, we went to see
the Ras-et-Teen, built by Mohammed Ali. It now
belongs to Tewfik Pasha, and stands in the island of
Pharos, which is connected with the mainland by the
old causeway called the Heptastadium. It is much
like all other palaces. It savours, however, too
much of the West, and too little of the East. It
exhibits more of French taste than Oriental splendour. It is furnished with great richness ; and the
parqueterie floors, inlaid with ebony, ivory, and
mother-of-pearl, are in their way handsome ; but the

view of the harbour from the windows and the
balcony is more worth seeing than anything inside.
There is nothing beyond this, and a few pleasant
drives along the bank of the Mahmoudieh Canal, or
to Ramleh, or under the acacia trees to the gardens
of the Khedive, to detain the visitor in Alexandria.
There is a ruin of much interest near Ramleh, the
fashionable watering-place of the wealthy Alex-
andrians, and where the air is said to be peculiarly
pure and bracing. The ruin is all that remains of
the famous temple of Queen Arsinöe as Venus, and
it stands on the promontory of Zephyrinus. When
King Ptolemy Euergetes left for his expedition to
Syria, his queen, the beautiful Berenice, made a vow
that if her husband returned in safety, she would
dedicate her hair to the gods. Her prayer was
answered, and she hung within the temple the golden
tresses that had adorned her head. But they were
not long permitted to form one of the ornaments of
the temple; they were stolen by some daring sacri-
legious thief from the sacred shrine. The priests
were troubled, the king was angry,—what was to be
done? The difficulty was at last solved by the
astronomers, who assured the king that no common
thief, but the gods themselves, had stolen the
beautiful tresses, and that they were to be seen, a

new constellation, in the sky. They pointed to a
cluster of stars which they now separated from Leo ;
and the king, who perhaps had not been an observer
of the heavens, or who was pleased with the explanation of the theft, was satisfied, and the constellation
shines still in the sky.

BERENICE'S HAIR.

The hour had come for them to part,
   The king must leave for Syrian shore,
And so he caught her to his heart,
   And kissed her sweet lips o'er and o'er.

Her head within both hands he took,
   With all its wealth of golden hair,
Bright as the ripened corn that shook,
   And rippled in the summer air :

" O love, dear love," he fondly cried,
   " 'Tis death in life to part from thee ! "
She, smiling through her tears, replied,
   " My heart will follow after thee.

" Thou know'st full well it is not mine,
   It left this bosom long ago,
Tis thine, dear love, and only thine,
   In life or death, in weal or woe."

One last embrace, he left the room;
   One lingering look, he passed away ;
The sunlight darkened into gloom,
   A cloud fell on the cloudless day.

The court with armèd men was filled,
  Glittered the spear, and flashed the shield,
At sound of trump each heart was thrilled,
  And legions burned to take the field.

Before he crossed the palace gate,
  He raised a yearning look above,
Where Berenice lonely sat,
  Dear as his life, his wife, his love.

She saw him go; she bends her head,
  From her sad eyes the big tears fall,
And with a faint, low voice she said,
  "My love, my husband, and my all.

"Ye gods that dwell in yonder sky,
  And o'er the earth and man hold reign,
Look down on him with pitying eye,
  Bring Euergetes back again.

"Upon your altars will I lay
  All that I have or hold most dear,
Will pour libations day by day,
  Will slay for you the spotless steer.

"Only bring back my lord in peace,
  Victorious from this dreadful fight,
And prayers and incense shall not cease
  To rise and burn by day and night."

The months passed by—he came not yet;
  Her heart was bowed with anxious fears,
Her sweet blue eyes were often wet
  With sad and unavailing tears.

Were the gods deaf to all her prayers?
  Regardless of her grief and woe?

Or did they mock her anxious cares,
  The tears that from her eyes would flow?

She sought once more the sacred fane,
  Where priests in fair white robes were drest,
And there she knelt and vowed again
  To sacrifice what she held best.

She loosed the fillet from her hair,
  Its fragrance made the day more sweet,
And sunshine seemed to fill the air,
  As showered the ringlets to her feet.

" I dedicate this hair," she said,
  "Which Euergetes praised as mine,
The glory of my woman's head,
  And lay it on this holy shrine."

The priest took in his hand the knife,
  The hair gleamed brighter than the sun,
Up in his eyes then smiled the wife,
  As fell the tresses one by one.

She hung the votive offering fair
  Within the inner sacred shrine ;
So brightly gleamed the golden hair,
  It made the temple walls to shine.

" Accept this offering," she said,
  " O'er Euergetes cast your shield,
Protect and guard his noble head,
  Send him victorious from the field."

The gods smiled on her from above,
  They listened to her pleading cry ;
And pleased with this new proof of love,
  They took the tresses to the sky.

They placed them in the vaulted blue,
  And when drew on the shades of even,
At once a constellation new
  Flashed in the purple depths of heaven.

And ever now, when falls the night,
  And cloudless are the depths of air,
Amongst the stars and planets bright
  Shines brightest Berenice's hair.

CHAPTER II.

E VERYTHING in these days is becoming
prosaic. You travel by railroad to Cairo.
Although there is no beauty of scenery along the line
to charm the eye and take it captive, there is much
that is novel and strange. You pass through a flat
country, level as a lake ; but the valley is green with
the young corn ; you see many a mud village, and
many a small town with its mosque and minarets ;
strings of camels pass by with their long necks, and
high heads, and patient looks ; donkeys and carts
laden with straw and Indian corn come and go ;
brown, bare-legged men are busy amongst the millet
or wheat ; and veiled women and naked children are
either busy in the fields, or idly basking in the sun.
You see for the first time the sakieh, which is a
water-mill of cogged wheels turned by an ox, and

14

which, at each turn of the wheel, works up a series
of earthen pitchers, which empty themselves into a
trough, and through this send the life-giving waters
through the thirsty land. Or perhaps it may be the
shadoof that is at work. This consists of a long pole,
very heavy at one end, and resting on a pivot. At
the other end is placed a bucket, which is let down
into the water and filled, and as the heavy end
descends, the bucket pours its contents into a small
trough. From this it is worked by the foot, and flows
into the channels, by which it is conveyed to the waiting fields. There is even a simpler method of raising
the water intended for irrigation. Two men stand in
the pool or stream, holding a bucket which is water-
tight between them, and which, as they swing it to and
fro, throws the water on to the bank, on which stands
a third man, ready to turn it into the proper channel.
This, no doubt, is the labour from which Moses tells
the Israelites they shall be free when they have
entered the land flowing with milk and honey. " For
the land, whither thou goest in to possess it, is not as
the land of Egypt, from whence ye came out, where
thou sowedst thy seed, and wateredst it with thy foot ;
but is a land of hills and valleys, and drinketh water
of the rain of heaven " (Deut. xi. 10, 11).

Presently, as the train hurries on its way, you come

upon that great and mighty river whose source has
always been the subject of mystery and wonder, and
which, throughout its course through sandy wastes
from its mouth up to the Atbara, which flows into it
from the mountains of Abyssinia, a thousand miles
from the sea, does not receive a single tributary.
This river is the beneficent cause of Egypt's fertility,
and without it Egypt would be a wilderness of sand.

There is little or no rainfall in Egypt. About an
inch falls in Cairo in the course of the year, and
higher up the Nile there is seldom any rain at all ;
so that the valley of Egypt depends altogether for its
fertility on the alluvial soil brought down at the
annual period of inundation by this river, from the
highlands of Abyssinia and Central Africa. Without
its beneficial waters, all would be barrenness and
famine. No wonder that, as they had "gods many,
and lords many," the Egyptians placed Nilus in their
pantheon, and worshipped at his shrine. The name
under which the river was personified and worshipped
as a god was Hapi, "the hidden," because its source
was unknown. The Egyptians call it the Sea, and as
the Sea it was known to the Hebrew prophets. Thus
we read in the prophet Nahum: "Art thou better than
populous No, that was situate among the rivers, that
had the waters round about it, whose rampart was

the sea, and her wall was from the sea?" (Nahum iii. 8.)

Sir William Dawson, in his *Modern Science in Bible Lands*, when speaking of the origin of the dark-brown mud deposited by the river, says that "the Nile mud is not mere clay or flinty sand, but a rich mixture of various minerals, capable of yielding to the roots of plants, alkalis and phosphates, and soluble silicates suited to nourish the richest crops." So that unless the river fail, as it did in the time of Joseph, when there was a famine in the land for seven years, the Nile, that through its gracious inundation every year washes down the rich soil from the highlands of Abyssinia, renews the face of the land, which needs no other aid to make it "bring forth and bud, that it may give seed to the sower, and bread to the eater."

Sir William Dawson, in the volume from which I have already quoted, tells us the reason of the delicious quality of the Nile water for drinking. "The rocks whose *débris* is borne down by the Blue Nile and Atbara, are old crystalline formations, yielding to the water no soluble ingredients. Consequently, the waters of the Nile are like those of a mountain stream, pure almost as rain water. Hence their celebrated 'sweetness,' in comparison with the more or less

brackish waters which issue from springs and wells in
the neighbouring desert. Thus we find a sufficient
cause of the freedom of the Nile waters from saline
matter, in its derivation from a country of siliceous
and crystalline rocks."

As we travelled along in the railway, it was with
the deepest interest, and with some measure of excitement, that we looked down from the windows of our
carriages in order to catch the first view of the Nile,
as its volume of rich brown waters glided placidly
along—that ancient river, thousands of years old,
winding past the modern railway of to-day.

But the feelings which are awakened by the Nile
are not allowed to slumber long, for as you approach
Cairo, you see the Pyramids of Ghizeh rising up sharp
and defined in outline on the edge of the desert—not
on the level of the river, but on a spur of the limestone
ridge that overlooks the valley, and against the blue
of a cloudless sky. Some say that this first view of
the Pyramids is disappointing, and that they are not
impressive ; but then we must remember that they
are eight or nine miles away, and that we have
nothing with which to compare their height, no
mountain or hill by which to measure them, and that
they stand on that level platform of sand, absolutely
alone, sepulchral monuments, magnificent in concep-

tion, and wonderful in execution. And is not the very thought, as you gaze upon them, impressive, that for four or five thousand years these royal tombs have stood there, in colossal grandeur, casting their shadows across the sands, before Rome had an existence, or European history began? To me, the view from a distance of these royal tombs was quite as impressive, nay, even more so, than the nearer view, when I stood under the mighty shadow that darkens the sunlight on the green plain below. But of this, more presently, when we visit these colossal sepulchres for the dead.

Cairo, or in the Arabic, Misr, is situated on the right bank of the Nile, at the foot of a spur of the Mokattam hills, and is but modern when we think of Memphis, or Heliopolis, or Thebes. Its history is not connected with the monarchies of the Hyksos or the Pharaohs, but with the Caliphs and Khedives. Founded in A.D. 969, by Gowher, a general of Aboo Tummeem, the first of the Fatimite dynasty who ruled in Egypt ; it was, at the end of this dynasty, fortified in 1171 by the brave and generous Saladin, so famous in the history of the Crusades ; and being situated at the apex of the Delta, it is the natural centre of Egypt, commanding the whole of the lower and upper country. It is the old part of the city that interests ; for the new quarter, with its boulevards, and clubs, and theatres, and hotels, is Paris over again, and is commonplace, modern, and fashionable. Leave the Ezbekyeh, and Shepherd's Hotel, and the shops, the cafés, the restaurants, and consulates, turn your back upon the public gardens, and enter by the Mooskee to the really Oriental part of the city, if you want to see Eastern life, and, in the words of Miss Martineau, to "surrender yourself to the most wonderful and romantic dream that can ever meet your waking senses." Oriental life, with all its phases of light and shade, colour and costumes, is seen at its best in the bazaars, which are native shops, these shops being recesses in the ground-floor of the houses which form the street. The shop is a space no larger than a cube of ten or twelve feet. A window closed with shutters serves the place of a door, and this the merchant takes down when he comes to business, and puts up when the day is over. He sits turbaned and cross-legged on the floor in front of his goods. Many of the streets of bazaars are covered over with canvas or planks, and you can make your purchases, and study Oriental costume under the grateful shade, and protected from the burning heat of the sun.

The houses in the old quarter of the city have the first floor advanced beyond the ground floor, and project over the street with delicately carved mushre-

beyceh lattice-work for the windows, and their picturesqueness at once attracts the eye of a stranger.
These, however, are disappearing fast, and are bought
by collectors, and carried off to adorn the houses of
the Western world. The unpaved streets are narrow,
and crowded with a restless throng, composed of all
peoples, nations, and languages. Here is to be seen
every shade of complexion in every variety of
Oriental costume. There are men in flowing robes
of the softest and most harmonious colours, wearing
on their head the kaffieh, or the fez, the white
turban, or the red tarboosh. Women are here in
black veils, which cover all their face but their eyes,
and wrapped in garments of dark blue or of black
cotton. Yonder is a lady with a veil of white muslin,
seated astride on a fine white donkey, which is led
by a servant richly clad, the lady herself wearing such
a large silk cloak, and so arranged, that she looks like
nothing so much as a distended bubble or an inflated
balloon. Here are men with water-skins or kenneh-
jars; others with " leben," or curdled milk; some with
dates, and oranges, and nuts ; and all ready to sell
their different wares, if you are only prepared to
buy. There are separate quarters for each kind of
merchandise. The carpet bazaar is very spacious,
and has compartments both above and below ;

and here are to be purchased the products of the looms of Syria and Persia, harmonious patterns from Turkey, and rugs from Tunis or Algiers, of the richest and most varied colours, and in all shades of red, and green, and blue. The gold and silversmiths' bazaar, which must be sought in the Sook-es-Saeegh, makes but little display of its precious goods ; but at your request the owners will bring you forth drawer after drawer from the back of their shops, filled with all manner of curiously wrought and glittering ornaments. Here you may buy chains, and bracelets, and earrings, collars for the neck, and anklets for the feet, and rings for the nose, many of them copied from beautiful and antique designs. Then there is a very tempting bazaar for those who love work in brass, from which they may carry off, at a price much lower than is asked at first, trays and cups, lamps and dishes, all beautifully engraved with camels and birds, and men and trees. Here, too, you will meet with cabinets of exquisitely carved work, and low stools of sandal-wood, inlaid with ivory and mother-of-pearl. But, indeed, there is nothing you can want that may not be found in the bazaars—saddles of every size and colour ; saddles for horses and donkeys ; saddles for ladies and gentlemen ; saddles studded with brass nails, or covered with silken braid, or embroidered in silver and gold. Then there is the shoe bazaar, where you will find walking shoes, or slippers for the room ; red slippers, turned up at the toes, much worn by the natives ; and velvet slippers in purple or blue, encrusted with beads and with pearls, or embroidered with silver and gold. If you wish to be carried back to the days of Haroon-en-Raschid ; if you want to be transported to the scenes of the enchanting stories of the " Arabian Nights," rub your " Aladdin's lamp," and go inside what still remains of old and picturesque Cairo, and your dreams will be realized, and your desires fulfilled.

No doubt Cairo is not what it was, even a few years ago. It is losing much of its picturesqueness by being Europeanized, and some of its most beautiful architectural monuments have been destroyed. But enough still happily remains to give pleasure and satisfaction. You will indeed meet with squalor and dirt, but you will also find grace and beauty. Even in unfrequented thoroughfares, in the stillness of streets where there are neither bazaars nor shops, there are marvellous effects of light and shade, a quaint corbel, a decorated door, an old mosque falling to decay, but whose graceful minaret, like a flame of fire, cleaves the sky, and soars away into the sunshine.

There is beauty everywhere—beauty of form and colour, beauty of architecture and decoration, which at once delights the eye, and appeals to the imagination.

CHAPTER III.

THE mosques are a distinct and interesting fea. ture of Cairo.   There are many which are well worth a visit.   The large mosques are open from early dawn till two hours after the sun sets ; but others are closed between the hours of morning and midday prayer.   The mosque El Azhar is open through the night, with the exception of the Mah. soorah, or chief place of prayer, which is screened off from the rest of the building.   Though the mosques are regarded with reverence, many as-semble there simply to lounge or to talk, while some spin or sew, eat, and even sleep there.   On the other hand, some of the richer mosques are closed when it rains, lest the people who wear no shoes—and there are many such among the poor—should soil the paved floor or the matting.   The features essential to a mosque are : the Sàhn-el-Gámah, or the open court ;

25

the Mehrab, or Kibleh, the niche in the principal wall
that shows the direction of Mecca ; the Mimbar, the
stone or wooden pulpit, always placed to the right
or south of the Kibleh. Besides these are the
Dikkeh, a platform with parapet, usually supported
by four columns ; and the Khoorsee, a desk for the
Korán. Outside the mosque is the open tank for
ablution, covered over by a canopy supported by
small columns ; and the chief external features of the
building are the rounded tower, and the minaret, from
which the Muezzin gives his calls to prayer ; and the
Mabkháreh, or tower, not unlike the minaret, but
without balconies, and the upper part of which is
perforated with holes, through which comes the smoke
of the incense which is burned at the time of prayer.
A mosque is generally attached to the tomb of the
founder, in order to give it dignity, and to surround
it with sacredness.   When a man of wealth wishes
to perpetuate his name, or show his gratitude to
Allah for some mercy, he builds a mosque, and
calls it after his own name ; hence the number of
mosques that are in Cairo, new ones still being
built, while the old monuments, rich in historical
interest, are permitted to fall into decay. If you
can perpetuate your own memory, why spend
money and labour in perpetuating the memory of

another ? This seems the guiding motive of the Oriental.

One of the mosques most worthy of a visit is the mosque of Sultan Hassan, built by En-nasr Hassan, and is a good specimen of Saracenic art in its highest and best style. After taking off your shoes, and putting on slippers, which are given you at the entrance of this, and all the mosques, for a trifling " backsheesh," you enter the great court, which is more than a hundred feet square, and the walls of which rise more than a hundred feet in height. So grand is its lofty porch, so beautiful the inner court, so graceful its arches, and so rich in all its details, and so striking the effect of the whole, that it is said that Sultan Hassan ordered the architect's hand to be cut off, lest he should build another to rival this splendid monument of Moslem architecture. No doubt this is but a myth ; for to cut off the architect's hand, and to leave the head which conceived and planned on his shoulders, would have been but blundering business on the Sultan's part. The oldest mosque in Cairo, and situated in the old quarter, is the mosque of Amer, the Arab conqueror. Founded in A.D. 643, it has been often rebuilt, and little of the original edifice remains. Many of the columns are fallen, but there is a fine colonnade consist-

ing of 230 pillars, and others are built into the outer
wall, and eight surround the open court. There are
two columns near the entrance about ten inches apart,
and no one but a true follower of the Prophet is
able to pass between them. There is one column
which is very curious ; the name of Mohammed, by
some strange freak of nature, may be traced in the
veins of the marble. We were shown a well in the
open court whose waters the guide assured us flowed
from the well "Zem Zem," at Mecca. There is a
tradition that when this mosque falls, Islam will fall
also and be no more.

Another mosque, only second in age to the mosque
of Amer, is that of Ahmed Ibn Tooloon, which is fast
falling into decay. Though not remarkable for
beauty, it has an interest of its own from the fact
that it shows how early was the existence of the
pointed arch ; for the date of this mosque, according
to two Kufic inscriptions on the walls, is A.D. 879—
that is to say, 300 years before the pointed arch
was adopted in England. It is supposed that we are
indebted to the Saracens for this form of architectural
beauty. The great mosque of El Azhar is not
only a mosque, but the principal university of the
Mohammedan world. You enter by the court of
the barbers, where you see the students submitting

their heads to the razor. There is an open court, paved, and surrounded by colonnades, with pointed arches supporting the walls. The sanctuary has a vast area, and has 380 columns, divided in nine rows, upon which rests a low roof that covers the whole space. Both this and the spacious outer court are crowded with students of all ages, from childhood upwards, grouped round the various teachers and professors, learning by heart, or writing, listening, or repeating. The number of students is said to be 10,000 or more ; and there could not have been fewer than two or three thousand the day we visited the mosque. Some of the pupils seem to take their learning easily, and talk and laugh as if they were at play. The foreign students are divided according to their nationality ; or if they are from Egypt, according to the province from which they come ; and the course of instruction includes not only the primary branches of education, but religion and logic, philosophy and law. Here meet scholars from all parts of the world, even from the interior of Africa ; and those who are too poor to pay are housed and fed at the cost of the endowment, and are taught without a fee.

Many of the mosques are rich in marble and mosaics, and some are carpeted, and several have numerous glass lamps suspended from the decorated roof. These, though they seem out of character with the building, and give it something of the appearance of a furniture shop, no doubt have a fine effect when the mosque is lighted for evening prayer. The mosque of Mohammed Ali is built in the Byzantine style, and contains the tomb of the founder. It is spacious and handsome, the outer court is of white marble, and the interior and the dome are effectively painted. The gallery is supported by columns of alabaster, but the mosque has no historical interest, and fails in impressing the imagination. I have seen many Moslems at prayer in their mosques and elsewhere, in the street, or the deck of the boat, where they spread out their prayer-carpet, and make their prostrations, indifferent to the presence of spectators. Prayer is with them a matter of prescribed words and postures, and seems to have nothing of the spontaneous utterance of the heart. They do not approach God through a Mediator; and I question whether they have any conception of sin, or of their need of forgiveness. Islam seems very much a religion of form without power,—of washings, and fastings, and festivals,—of that "bodily exercise" which "profiteth little." We may certainly learn from them the lesson of not being ashamed of our religion, and of the duty of confessing Christ before men.

While we do not stand at the corners of the streets in prayer,—while, indeed, we are directed to " go into our closets, and shut the door about us, and pray to our Father in secret,"—yet are we ever to " let our light so shine before men, that they may see our good works, and glorify our Father who is in heaven." The Prophet did not forbid women to attend public prayers in a mosque, but pronounced it better for them to pray in private. In Cairo, however, neither females nor young boys are allowed to pray with the congregation in the mosque, or even to be present there at any time of prayer. Formerly women were permitted at such times to enter, but were obliged to place themselves apart from the men, and behind the latter, because, as Sale has remarked, "the Moslems are of opinion that the presence of females inspires a different kind of devotion from that which is requisite in a place dedicated to the worship of God. Very few women in Egypt even pray at home."[1] Mohammedanism, by such exclusion of women from public worship, and, indeed, by its whole treatment of that sex which was meant by God to be a help-meet to man, dishonours man and degrades woman, and destroys the family relations which lie at the root of national life.

---

[1] Lane's *Modern Egyptians.*

CHAPTER IV.

THE Boulák Museum contains the richest collection in the world of Egyptian antiquities, and it transports you at once to the kingdoms and dynasties of the dim and distant past. We see the details of Egyptian life as it existed many thousand years ago. Here are engraved tablets, and votive statuettes found in mummy cases, sacred boats and shrines, and tables of offerings to the gods. Here are vases and urns, articles of furniture and dress. Here you see statues of kings, the sceptred dead of old, who held the world in awe, and whose names, inscribed on the granite, fix the date of their monuments. The bust of Menephtah, the Pharaoh of the Exodus, meets you in the large vestibule, where you look upon the likeness of him who "hardened his heart" against the judgments of God, and would not let His people go. Another bust bears the features of Tirkakah, king of the Ethiopians, mentioned in the 2nd Book of Kings, and also in the prophecies of Isaiah. Chephren, the builder of the second pyramid of Ghizeh, has a magnificent statue in the museum ; and there is a wooden statue, supposed to represent an old Egyptian sheykh, which commands general admiration from its life-like appearance and the vigour and attitude of the figure. Eyes have been inserted in the head, of opaque white quartz, the centre of the pupil being formed of rock crystal, and the eyelids of bronze. The whole effect is startling and impressive to a degree, as this old village chief of 4,000 years ago looks down upon you from his pedestal with clear and glittering eyes. The art and the luxury of the oldest civilization in the world is to be seen in the splendid gems and jewels taken from the .mummied dead,—chains and bracelets of gold, golden diadems and earrings ; scarabs in the same precious metal ; ornaments inlaid with lapis lazuli, turquoise and felspar, and handsome vessels of silver used in the service of religion. The scarabs, or sacred beetles, were placed inside the case of the mummy, because the beetle was the chosen emblem of a future life, and indeed of a resurrection from the dead. The scarab is very often engraven on the walls of D

tombs and temples as the symbol of immortality; and
no doubt it was adopted as the symbol of a future
life from the habits of this insect. The beetle, when
the time approaches for laying its eggs, deposits
them on the moist soil on the banks of the Nile,
which it forms into a round ball ; and this being
done, it pushes the little globe up the steep, and
rolls it away to the sands, which often lie some
distance off. Having reached the sands, it hollows
out a grave, in which it buries itself and the ball of
clay containing its eggs. There in due season the
eggs produce each a chrysalis, and from this chrysalis
emerges a winged beetle, which flies to and fro
in the sunshine. Now, in this life emerging from
the grave and gate of death, the old Egyptians saw
a symbol of resurrection, and hence they placed
the scarab—the beetle regarded by them as sacred—
with wings extended in the mummy case, and for
the same reason they engraved its form on their rings
or cut it on their seals. Numbers of these scarabs,
many thousand years old, cut in stone, or wood, and
found in the mummy cases, are offered for sale by the
Arabs; and there are few travellers who do not
purchase some to carry with them home.

But of all the objects of interest in the Boulák
Museum, the most impressive and interesting to me

were the mummies of Seti the First, the second king of the 19th dynasty, and son of Rameses the First; and the mummy of his son Rameses the Second, the Pharaoh of the oppression. The king under whom Joseph rose to honour was till lately supposed to be Apepi; but since the recent discoveries made by M. Naville, at Bubastis, and the finding of a headless statue of a king of Egypt, called " Rai-an," or " Ra-ian," Egyptologists believe that this was the name of Joseph's Pharaoh. If so, he must have been a Shepherd king of the 16th dynasty, anterior to Apepi. He could not have been a king of the 15th dynasty, for the names of the kings of this dynasty are, I believe, known. The Hyksos, or Shepherd kings, were a horde of barbarians from Asia, who conquered Egypt, and who, according to Dr. Brugsch, lived 1,750 years before the Christian era.

Apepi was a king of the 17th dynasty. This period is known as the Middle Empire, and was in existence before the time of Abraham. When the Hyksos were expelled, the 18th dynasty succeeded —the dynasty of Thothmes and Amenophis. The 19th dynasty begins with Rameses the First, father of Seti the First, whom Mariette places 1,462 years before Christ. Seti sought to earn a legitimate title to the throne by marrying Tua, the granddaughter of

Amenophis the Third; for in Egypt a noble family might be perpetuated through the female line. Pharaoh was the title of all these kings, and is the Hebrew form of the Egyptian Perau, or Phra. It signifies the "great house," or "high gate." The idea survives in the title of the Sultan—"the Sublime Porte."

Looking at the mummy of Seti the First, we see all that remains of a king mighty in his day, and who carried his conquests into Asia. But war was not the only thought in his mind. He sought the improvement of the country, and he made the first canal between the Nile and the Red Sea. His tomb, known as Belzoni's, is one of the most magnificent of the "tombs of the kings" at Thebes. You gaze upon his embalmed face, and you see that it is marked by lines of beauty and intellect. The face is oval, the nose aquiline in shape, the forehead not high but broad, the upper lip long, and the chin rounded and firm. Standing there, we look at no common man, and one who lies before you after the long sleep of more than a thousand years.

By the side of Seti is the mummy of his greater son, Rameses II., the Sesostris of the Greek historians, and the Oxymandias of the Persians. He was the monarch under whom Upper Egypt rose to its greatest pre-eminence in war, and in arts, and wealth

He has left behind him magnificent temples and colossal statues, and the name of no other king is so often met with on monuments as his. He carried successful war into Libya and Ethiopia, into Persia and Scythia, among the Armenians of the East and the Lycians of Asia Minor ; and a memorial of his victories in Palestine may be seen on the tablet at the mouth of the Nahr-el-kelb, the Dog River, near Beyrout. This is the Pharaoh of the oppression ; and his sister it was who, in her compassion, and struck by the beauty of the infant Moses, took the child from the ark of bulrushes, and brought him up as her own son. How strange it is to gaze upon his face, the face into which Moses often looked, when he was a child in his splendid court, or when, as a .man, he boldly confronted him as the oppressor of the Hebrew nation ! There he lies before you, still and calm, with an expression, if somewhat sensual, yet full of dignity and pride. It is an old man that you see, for he reigned sixty-seven years, sharing in his father's throne while yet but a boy, and he was a hundred years old when he died. A few hairs are on the temples, once white, but now become yellow through the process of embalming, and at the back of the head the hair is thick. The hands, with their fingers swollen at the joints, show that he was a sufferer from gout. The forehead is high, the eyes sit closely together, the cheek bones are prominent, and the nose is long and thin and curved, and the lips are full, while they are parted enough to show the teeth, which are still white. From the statues of this king, we learn that he must have been very handsome, while they all have a look of tenderness, which is blended with an expression of majesty and pride. The story of the finding of the mummy of Seti I. and of Rameses II., and other mummies of kings and queens now in the Boulák Museum, has been told in a most graphic manner by Mr. E. L. Wilson and Mr. John A. Painc, in the *Century Magazine* for May, 1887. I am sure it will interest all who have not read it. "Suspicion was aroused in the neighbourhood of Thebes by the sale of mummies, scarabei, small blue idols, and other precious things found in the tombs ; and as all such rifling the abodes of the dead is illegal, inquiry was made into the matter. It was discovered that four Arab brothers named Abd-er-Rasûl, who lived in the tombs close by the Rameseum, had found some tombs, broken into them, robbed them of their contents, and sold them to all willing to buy. Professor Maspero, in the year 1881, caused Ahmed Abd-er-Rasûl to be arrested, and he was imprisoned for two months at Kench. It was in vain that he was entreated and threatened, and that the bastinado was used as a last resort : he steadily refused to disclose the secret. But his brother Mohammed was more open to persuasion, and yielded under the promise of a large backsheesh to tell all he knew ; and on July 5th, 1881, Professor Maspero sent Brugsch Bey from Cairo to Deir-el-Bahari, with instructions to act for him in the matter. To reach the tomb it was necessary to climb a mountain slope, to scale a high limestone cliff, and there behind a great rock a shaft about six feet square was found, sunk about some forty feet. At the foot of this a passage ran westward for twenty-five feet, and then northwards into the heart of the mountain, terminating in a sepulchral chamber twenty-three feet by thirteen in extent, and about six feet high."

"Finding Pharaoh," Brugsch Bey told Mr. Wilson, "was an exciting experience. It is true I was armed to the teeth, and my faithful rifle, full of shells, hung over my shoulder ; but my assistant from Cairo, Ahmed Effendi Kemil, was the only person with me whom I could trust. Any one of the natives would have killed me willingly, had we been alone, for every one of them knew better than I did that I was about to deprive them of a great source of revenue. But I exposed no sign of fear, and proceeded with the work. The well cleared out, I descended, and began

the exploration of the underground passage. Soon
we came upon cases of porcelain funeral offerings,
metal and alabaster vessels, draperies and trinkets,
until, reaching the turn in the passage, a cluster of
mummy-cases came into view in such number as to
stagger me. Collecting my senses, I made the best
examination of them I could by the light of my
torch, and at once saw that they contained the
mummies of royal personages of both sexes ; and yet
that was not all. Plunging on ahead of my guide, I
came to the chamber, and there, standing against the
walls or lying on the floor, I found even a greater
number of mummy-cases of stupendous size and
weight. Their gold coverings and their polished
surfaces so plainly reflected my own excited visage,
that it seemed as though I was looking into the faces
of my own ancestors. The gilt face on the coffin of
the amiable Queen Nefert-ari seemed to smile upon
me like an old acquaintance. I took in the situation
quickly with a gasp, and hurried to the open air, lest
I should be overcome, and the glorious prize, still
unrevealed, be lost to science. It was almost sunset
then. Already the odour which arose from the tomb
had cajoled a troupe of slinking jackals to the neighbourhood, and the howl of hyenas was heard not far
distant. A long line of vultures sat upon the highest

pinnacles of the cliffs near by, ready for their hateful work. The valley was as still as death. Nearly the whole of the night was occupied in hiring men to help remove the precious relics from their hiding-place.

"There was but little sleep in Luxor that night. Early the next morning, three hundred Arabs were employed under my direction—each one a thief. One by one the coffins were hoisted to the surface, were securely sewed up in sail-cloth and matting, and then were carried across the plain of Thebes to the steamers awaiting them at Luxor. Two squads of Arabs accompanied each sarcophagus—one to carry it, and a second to watch the wily carriers. When the Nile overflow, lying midway of the plain, was reached, as many more boatmen entered the service and bore the burden to the other side. Then a third set took up the ancient freight, and carried it to the steamers. Slow workers are these Egyptians, but after six days of hard labour, under the July sun, the work was finished.

"I shall never forget the scenes I witnessed when, standing at the mouth of the shaft, I watched the strange line of helpers while they carried across the historical plain the bodies of the very kings who had constructed the temples still standing, and of the very priests who had officiated in them—the temple of

Hatshapsu nearest ; away across from El-Gûrneh ;
further to the right, the Ramesseum, where the great
granite monolith lies face to the ground ; further
south, Medinet Abû, a long way beyond the Deir-el-
Medineh ; and there the twin Colossi, or the vocal
Memnon and his companion ; then beyond all, some
more of the plain, the line of the Nile, and the Arabian
hills far to the east and above all; and with all, slowly
moving down the cliffs and across the plain, or in
the boats crossing the sea, were the sullen labourers
carrying their antique burdens.   As the Red Sea
opened and allowed Israel to pass across dry-shod,
so opened the silence of the Theban plain, allowed
the strange funeral procession to pass,—and then all
was hushed again.

" When we made our departure from Luxor, our late
helpers squatted in groups upon the Theban side, and
silently watched us.   The news had been sent down
the Nile in advance of us.   So when we passed the
towns, the people gathered on the quays, and made
most frantic demonstrations.   The fantasia dancers
were holding their wildest orgies here and there ; a
strange wail went up from the men, the women were
screaming and tearing their hair, and the children
were so frightened I pitied them.   A few fanatical
dervishes plunged into the river and tried to reach us;

but a sight of the rifle drove them back, cursing us as they swam away. At night fires were kindled and guns were fired.

"At last we arrived at Boulák, where I soon confirmed my impression that we had indeed recovered the mummies of the majority of the rulers of Egypt during the 18th, 19th, and 21st dynasties, including Rameses II., Rameses III., King Pinetem, the high priest Nebseni, and Queen Nefert-ari, all of whom are now at Boulák, arranged pretty much as I found them in the long-hidden tomb. And thus our museum became the third, and probably the final, resting-place of the mummy of the great Pharaoh of the oppression.",

Wonderful, is it not, to think of this discovery of the mighty dead of old ? and wonderful is it to stand in the presence of these historical kings who lived so long ago, and whose bodies have been disinterred that we may be taught something of the history of past ages, and have the truth of Holy Writ confirmed. We may be quite certain that "whatever record leap to light, *this* never shall be shamed." Egyptologists differ as to the period when Rameses reigned. Brugsch gives as the date B.C. 1407 ; Mariette, 1405 ; Lepsius, 1388 ; Bunsen, 1352 ; Poole, 1283. But the chronology of Egypt is still in a state of uncertainty, and cannot be settled with our present means of information. Manetho, a priest under the first two Ptolemies, between 300 and 250 years B.C., wrote in Greek a history of the Pharaohs, from the sacred records of Heliopolis. Some fragments of this history, and a catalogue of thirty royal dynasties, from Mena, or Menes, down to Nectanebo, who lived, according to Brugsch, B.C. 378, have been preserved through Josephus. The Egyptians themselves make extravagant claims to antiquity. Herodotus, who visited Egypt about 450 years B.C., tells us, in his interesting history, that the priests at that time claimed for their nation, from their first king, Mena, to Seti the First, an existence of 234 generations, or more than 11,000 years; and he says that during this time "no god had ever appeared in human form;" and beyond this Mena, was the mythical age of the gods. Some believe that Mena himself was a mythical personage, a personification of the two Misors, the Hebrew Misraim, or provinces of Upper and Lower Egypt. Indeed, chronology is in such an uncertain condition that Egyptian scholars vary in their estimates as much as 3,000 years,—the first Pharaoh, Mena, according to Boeckh, lived 5702 B.C.; according to Rawlinson, 2450. As to Bible chronology, theologians are divided between the longer period allowed by the Septuagint, which places the creation of man B.C. 5400, and the shorter system of the Hebrew text, which places it 1,400 years later. We must not form a hasty judgment on this vexed question, but wait until further light is thrown on the whole subject. It is a happy thing that the truth of the Bible does not depend on chronology,—that the witness to its history and doctrines is unassailable, and that it fears no discoveries from any of the sciences, so that we may rest calm in the assurance that heaven and earth shall pass away, but that the words of this Book shall never pass away.

RAMESES II. (*Bouldk Museum*).

I stand and gaze upon thy mummied face,
   Thou who didst deem thyself a demi-god,
   Before whom monarchs paled, and kings were awed,—
Thou greatest scion of a royal race,
Lying so still within death's grim embrace.
   And art thou he who carried wars abroad,
   Who shook the trembling nations with thy nod,
And brought them to thy feet to pray for grace?

Did Moses look into that face so cold,
   Those eyes so vacant, and that form so still?
What! Did he brave thee in the days of old,
Defying in God's name thy passionate will,
   Which in hard bondage did the Hebrews hold,
Till life was death, and death itself no ill?

CHAPTER V.

WE made during our brief stay at Cairo, and before ascending the Nile, an excursion to the Pyramids. We had seen them on a former visit to Cairo, but they cannot be seen too often, so impressive are they, and so suggestive of solemn thought and inquiry. We drove through the new quarter of Cairo, called, from its founder, Ismailia, and, crossing the Nile by the Kasr-el-Nil bridge, passed by the road constructed by the Khedive, and which leads from Ghizch to the Pyramids. It is a drive from the Ezbekyeh of about seven and a half miles. We had a view of these colossal monuments nearly all the way to their foot, and the sunshine steeped them in a brilliant golden light. Few appreciate the Pyramids on a first view : they arc unable to take in their size and proportions ; and this

arises, as I have said, from the want of some point
of comparison by which to measure their immensity.
They rise from the sands of the illimitable desert in
solitary grandeur,— the only mountains that cast
their shadows over the waste. But the longer you
look, the more they grow upon the eye, and the more
they affect the imagination. " One sees in them," as
Mariette says, " the most lofty, the most durable, the
most stupendous monuments under heaven that have
ever been erected by the hand of man." The three
great Pyramids are the tombs of Cheops, of Chephren, and of Mycerinus ; the smaller ones—for there
are several—are the sepulchres of ancient kings and.
their families. The Great Pyramid was formerly 479
feet high, but at present measures only about 453
feet ; its base covers an area of nearly twelve acres.
Built of nummulitic limestone, the Pyramids were
covered originally with a smooth coating of red
granite, but this has entirely disappeared ; and they
once terminated in a sharp point. They were robbed
of their granite casing to enrich the palaces and
mosques of Cairo, by the Saracens, the Greeks, and
the Romans. Herodotus says that one hundred
thousand workmen, changing every three months for
ten years, were employed in making a causeway for
the conveyance of stones, and that twenty years more

were spent in building the Pyramid itself.[1] It cost
1,600 talents of silver, or £200,000 sterling. Herodotus records that 1,600 talents of silver were spent
in buying radishes, onions, and garlic for the workmen. Does not this recall to the mind the murmurs
of the Israelites, when, in their march through the
desert, their thoughts flew back to the abundance
they had left? "We remember the fish, which we
did eat in Egypt freely; the cucumbers, and the
melons, and the leeks, and the onions, and the
garlic."[2] Abd-el-Latif, an Arab physician of Bagdad, who wrote in the early part of the 13th century,
says that "the most admirable particular of the
whole is the extreme nicety with which the stones
have been prepared and adjusted; their adjustment
is so precise that not even a needle or a hair can be
inserted between any two of them; they are joined
by a cement laid on to the thickness of a sheet of
paper." Now, the granite casing being removed, the
smoothness of surface has disappeared. I do not
know that it will much help those who have never
seen them, to realize the dimensions of the Great

[1] "Thus," according to the calculation of Birch, "four million
men were employed on this work alone, while it required seven
millions more to build the Pyramid itself."

[2] Numbers xi. 5.

Pyramid, to say that it is fifty feet higher than the dome of St. Paul's, and more than twice as high as the central tower of York Minster. The area that it covers is equal to the area of Lincoln's Inn Fields, and it is computed to have contained 6,848,000 tons of solid masonry. It may be asked, " What was the motive of these stupendous monuments ? " Some, like Mr. Piazzi Smyth, have given them an astronomical intention, and have constructed from them an elaborate scheme by which they endeavour to prove that the Great Pyramid of Ghizeh was intended to "perpetuate a knowledge of scientifically ascertained natural standards of weight, measure, and capacity." But Mariette and other learned Egyptologists have come to the conclusion that the Pyramids, great and small, "were tombs, massive, entire, everywhere hermetically sealed, even in their most carefully constructed passages ; without windows, without doors, without external openings of any kind."

Inside the Great Pyramid is a series of " inextricable passages and rooms." These were intended to deceive any who might wish in the future to violate the pyramid, and find the royal mummy ; for the various chambers and corridors, the blocks of granite barring the way, the mysterious well, the object of which was a puzzle to the discoverers, were all meant

to obstruct the way to the place where the sarcophagus of the dead king was placed. Such, then, was
the purpose of the Pyramids : they were tombs, and
nothing else—gigantic tombs, intended to portray
the belief of the builders in the shortness of the
life that now is, and the duration of the life that is
to come. " The Egyptians," says Diodorus, " call
their habitations hostelries, because of the short space
of time during which they sojourn there ; whilst they
speak of their tombs as eternal abodes."

According to Lepsius, the Pyramids were graves.
The plan of construction, as laid down by Lepsius,
is as follows :—" When a new king ascended the
throne, he began at once to build a pyramid. The
site having been chosen, the ground was levelled,
and a slanting shaft was bored out of the solid rock,
and at the end of this shaft a rectangular chamber
was made, which was intended to hold the sarcophagus containing the king's body. On the flat
side a comparatively small building was made, the
outsides of which were steep steps. If the king died
at this stage of the work, he was laid in his sarcophagus, and the steep steps of the little building
were filled up with triangular pieces of stone, and
so its sides became smooth, and the pyramid, though
little, was complete. If, on the other hand, the king

lived another year, a second layer of stones was built on to the four sides; but the layers became gradually smaller. When the king died, no further layers were added, and the pyramid was finished either by the steps being filled up with exactly fitting pieces of stone, or another layer of stones was added, and then the edges of the stones were chiselled away until each side of the structure was perfectly smooth. It is perfectly evident that such a tomb might well be considered everlasting, for it was inaccessible to the attacks of the elements, and its destruction would be a very difficult piece of work, even for modern nations. The size of a pyramid, then, varied generally with the length of the king's life; but vanity, and a desire to possess the largest pyramid, may have induced a king to add two layers, or even more, for each year of his life."

Here we have another side to this question—"the motive of the Pyramids"—may there not have been a good deal of self-glorification and pride in the construction of these immense mausoleums for the reception of the body of a king after death? And the walls, covered with the triumphs and deeds of the king, his victories over his enemies, his meritorious actions—do they not tell a tale of self-exaltation, and a supreme human pride? And at what a cost

of human life these huge mountains have been built,
—the labour of hewing out the stones in the Arabian
hills at Assouan, and conveying them from their distant quarries, being greater than we can even conceive. If those walls could speak, what a story of
sorrow and oppression, of tears and of blood, they
would be able to tell! The treasures of money spent
in their erection were great, but the treasure of human
lives was far greater during the years required for the
building of works of which it has been said : "All
things dread Time, but Time dreads the Pyramids."

Not far from the Great Pyramid, and on a lower
level of the slope of sand, rises the Sphinx above the
solitary waste—a huge granite figure, cut out of the
solid rock, now entirely laid bare, and to be seen
in all its gigantic proportions. This Sphinx unites
the body of a lion to the face of a man, and represents intellect with physical strength ; and this
thought underlies all figures of the Sphinx, whether
they have the head of a man, as at Ghizeh, or the
head of a ram, as at Karnak. The former are called
Andros-sphinxes, the latter Krios-sphinxes. An inscription at Edfou explains the meaning of these
composite forms. We learn from it that they originally symbolized the struggle of the god Horus, son
of Osiris and Isis, with the evil spirit Typhon, when,

in order to avenge the death of Osiris, he assumed
the shape of a lion with a human head, and slew the
foe. The Sphinx of the Pyramids is 65 feet high,
and 11 feet 7 inches across the face, the other features being in proportion. The body is 140 feet in
length, and the paws 50 feet. It is very difficult to
estimate its size from below, and perhaps you judge
of it most accurately when an Arab runs up the
figure, and seats himself on its neck. He looks but
a pigmy there—a sparrow sitting alone on the house-
top. The face is much mutilated, and it is difficult
to conceive what beauty it possessed when fresh
from the sculptor's chisel, bearing the royal helmet
on its head, and its beard flowing from its chin.
Between its paws religious processions used to march
to the temple; and on the altar, sheltered by its
breast, sacrifices were offered, whose savour rose to
its nostrils, which were supposed to be gratified by
the incense. Abd-el-Latif speaks of the face as
being very beautiful, the mouth as graceful and
lovely; and he mentions that the red paint on the
face was fresh and vivid. It is called in the hieroglyphics, Hor-em-Khoo—"Horns in the horizon,"
which means the Sun-god, the sun being the symbol
of all the Egyptian kings. The modern Arabs give
it a name of their own—Aboo-el-Hol—" the father

of Terror." There has this figure stood looking over
the valley of the Nile, over the illimitable desert,
with its face turned towards the rising sun—stood
there tranquil and immovable, in an attitude of
majestic repose, while dynasties have changed, and
kingdoms have been overthrown, while Pharaohs
passed along the stage and vanished, and Persian
kings carried their wars into the country, and Hebrew
patriarchs and lawgivers worshipped the one true
God, and Roman emperors came and conquered,
and Greek philosophers made discoveries in the
sciences, and Christian anchorites sought refuge in
the deserts from the world, and men of learning and
travellers from all countries have come to gaze upon
the face so impassive and calm. And there this
monstrous creature may still " stare right on with
calm, eternal eyes," across the river, across the wilderness of sand, till time shall be no more, and the
heavens and the earth that now are shall pass away
amid terrible convulsions, and give place to the new
which are to come. But even under the shadow of
the Pyramids all is not solemn or sad. There are
merry voices heard—voices of Arabs who would
fain help you to climb to the top of these venerable
monuments ; voices of boys asking for backsheesh ;
voices of traders in forged antiques, begging you

to buy their manufactured wares. There is much noise, and shouting, and struggling, shouts of laughter and merriment, and a strange medley of many languages. You are amazed ; you wish to be alone with nothing but the desert and the sky, and the Pyramids towering above you ; but it is well to be patient, for to lose your temper would do no good ; and, after all, these Arabs, if you take them rightly, are fellows of infinite good nature, and will afford you interest and amusement as fresh as they are novel.

CHAPTER VI.

AMIDST a field of sugar-cane, within a short drive of Cairo, rises a single column, all that remains of the once renowned city of On, the City of the Sun, the Hebrew Beth-shemesh, the Gentile Heliopolis. Heliopolis was the seat of a celebrated university, a school of learning and a centre of knowledge, to which resorted the wise men of Greece. Here, as we read in *The Cities of Egypt*, was wont to come, once in five hundred years or more, the mysterious Arabian bird, the phœnix. The winged wonder had no sooner settled than he made his nest, only to set it in flames and perish, when, lo! from his ashes arose a new phœnix, which spread his red and golden wings and flew away to the unknown land whence his parent came.

Here, where stood, in far-past ages, a populous city,

with its palaces and temples, and dromos of sphinxes, there are now only mounds, traces of massive walls, and fragments of masonry. The obelisk is of red granite, and is 68 feet high. It bears the name of Osirtasen I., the second king of the 12th dynasty, and it stood before the Temple of the Sun at the end of a long avenue of sphinxes. There is only one obelisk that is older—the one discovered by Lepsius in the Necropolis at Memphis. This one has stood for nearly 4,000 years in solitary grandeur, and was there when Abraham and Sarah went down into Egypt to sojourn for a time, the famine being sore in the land of Canaan. It was here that Joseph found his wife, and married Asenath, the daughter of Potipherah, the priest of On ; and no doubt his marriage was celebrated with all the splendour and pomp of a splendid age. Manetho says that it was here that Moses was "taught in all the learning of the Egyptians." The Hebrews, in their hours of work or of leisure, often looked upon this column, and read and deciphered the hieroglyphics with which it is covered. And to this city our Lord was most probably brought by His parents when they sought a refuge in Egypt from the cruelty of that Herod who sought the young Child's life. Close to Heliopolis there is a sycamore fig-tree, called the Tree of the

Virgin—for, according to a Coptic legend, Mary rested here with Joseph and her first-born son ; and it is not improbable that the tradition may be true. It is not at all unlikely that the holy family should seek refuge in a spot so connected with the history of their nation. Close to the Virgin's Tree is the miraculous fountain, which, according to another Coptic tradition, was once salt, but which became sweet when Mary bathed the infant Jesus in its waters. Whether a wish to believe interesting traditions will carry all so far as to credit this legend is doubtful. But in Egypt, as in the Holy Land, we must often doubt where an unquestioning faith would be delightful. Be this as it may, we know from history that in the celebrated university of Heliopolis, Solon and Pythagoras and Plato studied, and Strabo was shown the house where the latter resided ; and they must often have admired the sculpture, and interpreted the inscriptions of this monument of Osirtasen. The bees had not then covered the hieroglyphics with their nests, and the granite shaft stood in all the freshness of its beauty, though even then many years had passed away since its erection at On. And now all is waste and desolation where once stood a famous and populous city, a few green fields recovered from the sands cover the monuments of the dead.

Every one who goes to Cairo visits the Citadel to see the sunset—visits it more than once ; for the splendid prospect cannot be seen too often. The great city lies below you with its domes and cupolas and minarets, with its gardens and its palms and its moving throng of people ; here a procession of donkeys with their riders, there a string of camels with their burdens. The Nile, winding its way through yellow sands, gleams blue in the distance, and touches in its course many a green spot which owes its beauty and fertility to its waters. Far to the west, across the opulent river, and on the edge of the arid desert, the Pyramids of Ghizeh and Dashoor rise into the sky, coloured by the rays of the sun as he hastens to his setting. Yonder, to the right is a green plain, stretching away to the land of Goshen. The Mokattam hills are rosy in the lustrous light, and the Libyan mountains form a boundary to the beautiful view. You cannot visit the citadel without thinking of Mohammed Ali's treacherous deed of blood, and the massacre of the Mamelukes. The Mameluke Beys were a band of Circassian adventurers who had been brought into Egypt as slaves, in order to serve in the Sultan's army. They gradually rose to power, and the government of the country virtually passed into their hands. Mohammed

Ali came to Egypt as a volunteer in the service of the Sultan. He was jealous of the power of the Mamelukes, dreaded it, and wished himself for empire and authority. When he felt sure of the troops under his command, he invited the whole body of the Mamelukes to a splendid banquet; and after the festivities were ended, he parted from his guests with the usual courtesies. But the guests were caught in a trap. When they had mounted their horses in the court, and were about to leave the gates, they found them closed. As they were turning round to ride back to the pasha, a murderous fire was opened upon them from above. They saw at once that there was no escape; the pasha did not appear, the gates were closed, and the walls of the citadel were high. They were doomed. Man after man was shot down, and lay weltering in his blood. One alone escaped—Emin Bey. In the extremity of his despair, in his resolute determination not to be shot down like a dog, and in a forlorn hope that he might escape the cold-blooded treachery of the pasha, he forced his horse to the parapet, and the good steed seconding his master's wish, he leaped into the narrow street below, and fled to the tents of some Arabs that were pitched about two miles from the city, where he found an asylum, until he was able to leave the country. The butchery

—for butchery it was—took place on the 1st of March, 1811, and the number who were slain in the citadel amounted to 500. Many more of inferior rank were destroyed in the city, and the power of the Mamelukes crushed for ever. Mohammed Ali's slaughtered victims were replaced by an army of Turks and Circassians, on whose loyalty and devotion he could rely. But though he gained his object, he rightly suffered in the estimation of all civilized nations by this infamous deed of treacherous barbarity. In some accounts of the incident, the horse that took the leap is said to have been killed, while Emin Bey escaped ; but I prefer to believe the story as narrated above, and to think that the noble steed did not lose his life, and was his master's friend and companion for many a long day.

CHAPTER VII.

WE left Cairo for our passage up the Nile
on January 3rd, and joined the steamer
Rameses at 10 a.m., just above the new iron
bridge Kasr-el-Nil. The *Rameses* is the largest of
Messrs. Cook's steamers, and is fitted up with every
convenience, such as electric bells and a good supply
of baths—with all, indeed, that can make a Nile
voyage agreeable ; and the only thing wanting to
make the boat perfect is the electric light, which
might easily be supplied, and would add much to
the comfort of the passengers. As we sailed up the
river we passed houses and gardens, palaces and
mosques, shaded by the sycamore and the palm.
Then came the Citadel, with the slender minarets of
the mosque of Mohammed Ali ; and in the distance

was the long outline of the Mokattam hills. On the western shore rose the Pyramids, apparently only a short distance off, though in fact some miles intervened, so clear and transparent was the air. Our first excursion from the boat was made from Bedreshein, where the boat halted, in order that the passengers might visit Mitrahenny and Sakkarah. We found donkeys and men awaiting us, and mounting, we rode through the village of Mitrahenny, situated on an arid mound, blocks of granite being scattered here and there, and the foundations of old walls appearing through the surface of the soil ; these, and a hollow space, once the site of the temple of Phtah, the Greek Vulcan, with some crumbling bricks and broken pottery, being all that remains of the once magnificent Memphis, the chief city of Egypt, and the residence of the Pharaohs. The splendour of this ancient capital has departed, the glory of its palaces and temples is no more. Who can ride through the palm groves which cast their cool shadows over these crumbling mounds, the only vestiges of its former greatness, and not recall the words of the prophet Jeremiah?—"O thou daughter dwelling in Egypt, furnish thyself to go into captivity : for Noph (Memphis) shall be waste and desolate without an inhabitant" (Jer. xlvi. 19).

A short ride from Mitrahenny brings us to the
colossal statue of Rameses II., more than 48 feet
high, and formed of polished siliceous limestone.   It
used to stand before the temple of Phtah, and the
last time I saw it, in 1886, it was lying on its face
in the mud, beneath the palms ; but even in this prostrate and partly hidden condition, the grandeur of the
head and the beauty of the face could be recognised.
It has since then, however, been raised by the energy
and perseverance of an English officer from its debased position, and placed horizontally on a platform
within a wooden hoarding, to which you ascend by a
few steps, and get a good view of the features of
this Pharaoh of the 19th dynasty—the Pharaoh who
demanded the usual tale of bricks from the Israelites,
and denied them straw.   The statue, discovered about
1820, was given to the British Museum by Mohammed Ali, but has not been removed to England,
doubtless because of the expense.   I think it is
better where it is, lying under the shadow of the
palms, the sole surviving vestige of the glory of
Memphis, the city of Mena, the oldest of Egyptian
kings.

Leaving this colossal statue of the celebrated
conqueror of the 19th dynasty, we rode under the
shelter of the trees to Sakkarah, a village which gives

its name to the necropolis which extends four miles and a half along the edge of the desert ; and our pathway lay among fragments of granite and crumbling walls of brick lying among the sands. As you think of this vast city of the dead, extending for miles with its crumbling mounds that indicate ancient tombs, you are reminded of the question of the murmuring Israelites on their journey through the wilderness, as they impatiently said to Moses, " Because there were no graves in Egypt, hast thou brought us to die in the wilderness ? " There are eleven pyramids on the sands of Sakkarah, the most remarkable of which is called the Step-pyramid, from being built in six stages ; and if tradition may be trusted, it dates from the 1st dynasty, and is therefore the most ancient monument, not only in Egypt, but in the world. Not far from the Step-pyramid is the Serapeum, discovered by M. Mariette in 1860, his attention having been drawn to the spot by a passage in Strabo, in his description of Memphis. " One day," he says, " being attracted to Sakkarah by my Egyptological studies, I perceived the head of one of these same sphinxes (mentioned by Strabo as only partially covered by sand) obtruding itself from the sand. This one had never been touched, and was certainly in its original position. Close by lay a

F

libation-table, on which was engraved in hieroglyphs
an inscription to Osiris-Apis. The passage in Strabo
suddenly occurred to my mind. The avenue which
lay at my feet must be the one that led up to the
Serapeum, so long and so vainly sought for." So he
" gathered together a few workmen, and the excava-
tion began. The first attempts were hard indeed, but
before long, lions and peacocks and the Grecian
statues of the dromos, together with the monumental
tablets or stelæ of the temple of Nectanebo, were
drawn out of the sand, and I was able to announce my
success to the French Government." Thus was begun
the discovery of the Serapeum. Apis, an incarnation of Osiris, returning to the earth after his death
as a sacred bull, bearing the mark of a white star on
his forehead, had a temple raised to his honour at
Memphis, and lived in a palace called the Apieum,
suitably fitted up by his worshippers for his residence,
and which had its hareem of cows. When he died he
was buried with suitable distinction, and his mummy
was placed in the Serapeum, a colossal structure
with its two pylons and its avenue of sphinxes. Of
the Serapeum all that remains are the subterranean
vaults, the burial-place of the sacred bulls. We
visited the third of these galleries, the only one now
accessible, the entrance to which slopes down from

the sands, and found ourselves in a large dark chamber, with others leading from it, in which are huge granite sarcophagi, each one the tomb of a dead apis. There are twenty-four of these, three only bearing an inscription, and engraven on them are the names of Amasis of the 26th dynasty, of Cambyses and Khebasch of the 27th dynasty. There is one that has cartouches, and this Mariette supposes to belong to one of the Ptolemies. " As to their dimensions, they measure on an average 7 feet 8 inches in breadth, by 13 feet in length, and 11 feet in height; so that, allowing for the vacuum, these monoliths must weigh one with the other not less than sixty-five tons each." [1] An immense slab of granite closes the sarcophagus like a lid ; and we marvel as we remember that these huge blocks were brought here from the quarries of Assouan, some 600 miles away. These subterranean tombs are seen by the light of candles, one of which each person who visits them carries in his hand, or better still by the light of magnesium wire, which the dragoman takes care to bring with him, that the vast subterranean vaults may be illuminated by the flash. We leave these galleries with the thought that no king or hero,

[1] Mariette : *Monuments of Upper Egypt*, p. 93.

no statesman, warrior, or poet, has tombs of such grandeur and magnificence as these sarcophagi made for the reception of the sacred bulls, and we see how the worship of the apis throws light upon the worship of the golden calf, and the words of the people one to another: " These be thy gods, O Israel, which brought thee up out of the land of Egypt ! "

From the Serapeum we went to the tomb of the priest Tih. This tomb is constructed on the same principle as all the tombs of ancient Egypt. The tombs of the ancient empire are thus described by Mariette : " The tombs were generally in the form of a mastabah, which is a sort of pyramid truncated near the base, and which from a distance presents the appearance of an enormous sarcophagus lid. The mastabah consists of three parts; viz.: (1) One or more chambers, sometimes with the addition of a serdab, a sort of narrow passage, concealed in the thickness of the masonry,—these chambers being accessible at all times through a doorway opening upon one of the streets of the necropolis ; (2) a vertical pit opening out of one of the chambers ; (3) a sepulchral chamber hollowed out in the rock, wherein the mummy reposes. The serdab never bears any inscription ; the chambers, on the contrary, are almost always decorated." In the tomb of Tih the decorations on the walls of the chambers represent the priest in his life, and not as in other tombs, as he passes in his mummy state through different scenes after death. The colours in this tomb are very bright and fresh, though I cannot say, as some have said, that they look as vivid as if the pictures were painted but yesterday. However, a little exaggeration may be allowed to a pardonable enthusiasm. The walls are a revelation of the life of the times. Here you see the priest, with his wife at his side, and his children near ; he is waited on by his servants ; women are dancing before him, and musicians playing, and singers singing for his amusement. There you see him shooting in the marshes, standing in a bark made of papyrus reeds ; beneath his boat are crocodiles and hippopotami, which his servants are trying to catch, and one of them has hooked a hippopotamus with a sort of harpoon.

But agricultural scenes are also depicted. Men are reaping and stacking the corn ; they are threshing it, and tying it into sheaves. Cows are wading through a ford, calves feeding in a meadow, and herdsmen leading a flock of goats ; and Tih is present at all these scenes, and you infer that he must have been a happy and prosperous proprietor of the olden time, and one who, like the lady of Shunem, "dwelt

amongst his own people." Each chamber has its
own especial interest, and taking us back into the
life of the distant past, proves that " there is nothing
new under the sun."

After leaving the tomb of Tih, we visited the tomb
of Phtah-Hotef, which consists of only one chamber
covered with sculptures referring to the presentation
of gifts to the dead man. Priests, chanting sacred
hymns, march before a procession of servants who
bring offerings, and place them on a table prepared
for the reception of votive oblations. Phtah-Hotef
himself receives the gifts, and carries to his lips a
vase containing one of the substances which figure in
the bringing in of the funeral gifts. All the pictures
in this tomb—the representations of the house and
farm, the cattle, the fields, the harvest, the ships, the
life of the dead man after death—illustrate the saying
of Diodorus, who, as mentioned before, tells us that
the Egyptians regarded their tombs as eternal abodes.
As to the mummy itself, it was always concealed with
the ritual of the dead in a chamber at the bottom of a
pit, hidden away from view, and the very entrance to
which was carefully concealed, so that no one may
ever pass through. Their great care was that the
dead should not be disturbed, and their tomb violated.
After a visit to the Pyramid of Onas, which has

been opened and cleared at the expense of the
Messrs. Cook, we returned to the steamer ; and the
boat anchored that night at Ayat, thirty-six miles
from Cairo.

CHAPTER VIII.

ON the next morning, early, the good ship *Rameses* pursued her course up the river, passing Beni-Souef, from which you catch a view of the dwarf pyramid of Meydoum, called by the Arabs the Haram-el-Khedab, or " the false pyramid," because the base stands on an artificial mound, and it looks as though it were formed of the rock itself, to which a rough sort of masonry has given the shape of a pyramid. We also passed Wasta, where is the railway junction for the fertile district of the Fayoum, and Beni-Souef, the chief town of the province, and the largest town in Upper Egypt. The pasha has a handsome-looking house here, and some slender minarets rising into the blue sky are seen above the groves of palms. We "tied up" at Maghaga for the night. There is a sugar factory here which we visited in the evening, walking about two miles under the lustre of the stars, and assisted by the light from some lanterns carried by men from the boat. The path led through fields of corn and lentils, and close to the Nile. The soil is very rich, and crops of sugar-cane are grown on the level between the rocks and the river for some distance along the banks. The tall, heavy-looking chimneys seem out of place amidst such surroundings, and contrast ill with the light and graceful minarets of the mosques. The factory is lighted by gas, and the engines were made at Paris. It was a strange and a weird scene. Hundreds of men and children are employed here. Some work from five in the morning until six in the evening Others work through the night. Numbers were lying about on the ground asleep, worn out by the day's labour, and overcome by the heat. As wood is scarce in the country, and charcoal cannot be had, burnt bones are used for refining the juice. The noise of the engines, the heat of the gas, the smell of the brown liquid running in troughs, the half-naked workmen, formed a combination of disagreeables which made one glad to beat a retreat as soon as possible, and it was pleasant to stand again

under the stars in the cool night air. Though the
factory belongs nominally to the Khedive, yet I
understand it is really in the hands of the Egyptian
bankers, who take the profits to pay off the Egyptian
bondholders.

There are several other sugar factories on the
Upper Nile, the one at Minieh giving employment
to about 2,000 people, and another large one at
Erment ; and they may be regarded as among the
great industrial resources of the country.

On the third day, Thursday, January 5th, we passed
some steep, rocky cliffs, on whose summit stands the
Coptic convent of "Our Lady, Mary the Virgin."
The limestone cliffs assume the most grotesque
forms ; and there are flights of steps here and there
on the rocks, down which the monks, at a signal
from the women and children on the outlook, used to
leap and run, and then throwing themselves into the
water, struggled on board the boat to ask for backsheesh. This unseemly custom was some years since
put an end to by the Coptic patriarch, much to his
credit.

Passing Minieh, where the viceroy has a palace,
well seen from the deck of the steamboat, we came to
Beni-Hassan (the children of Hassan), where we
stopped in order to visit the rock-cut tombs. We

found donkeys on the shore ready for mounting, and were almost torn to pieces by a rabble of men and boys, all urgent that we should take their particular beast, and greeting us with clamorous cries that " Telegraph " was "very good donkey," or "Ginger" a better, or that " Yankee Doodle " was best of all, or that " A 1 " went very fast. When we had, with some difficulty, been rescued from the clamorous crowd, we selected the beast that seemed good in our eyes, appealing to the dragoman, Mohammed, for his assistance. We then rode over the sands to Speos Artemidos—"speos" meaning a rock-hewn tomb— which is the first that is visited ; the name given it by the Arabs is "Stabl Antar." This tomb has the appearance of a temple more than a tomb, for it has a portico, and columns, and architraves cut into the face of the rock. Though it dates from a very early period, yet the architecture is more Grecian than Egyptian, for here we find the beautiful if slightly fluted Doric pillar. As these tombs date from a period little later than the age of the Pyramids, the influence of Greek art and sentiment cannot be suspected, although we have the shaft and the abacus, and "the roofs of some of the grottos are cut into a slight segment of a circle, in imitation of the arch," which Sir G. Wilkinson believes was probably known in Egypt at this early period. The colour on the basement of all the chambers is a deep red, " to give them the appearance of red granite," and the hieroglyphics on the walls are everywhere painted in green. On the walls of the various chambers are frescoes which represent the daily life of the people in these ancient days. Here you see herdsmen with their flocks ; men ploughing and reaping, hunting, and fishing, and wrestling, dressing flax, spinning, weaving, and cutting the nails of their toes. There are harpers with their harps, some women playing at ball, and others with disordered hair engaged in different games. Truly history repeats itself ; one age is but the repetition of another. Life in the ancient days, the days of old, is in many of its aspects what life is in this advanced nineteenth century. After the Speos Artemidos had been inspected, we again mounted our donkeys, and rode a little farther on to visit the two most interesting of the other fifteen rock-tombs—those called Ameni-Amen-emha and Knum-Hotef. On the way to these, the ruins of the roofless and ruinous village of Beni-Hassan were passed, the village having been de-stroyed by order of Mohammed Ali, because of the evil character of the inhabitants, murders having been frequent, and the place a haunt of robbers.

Soldiers coming over the hills surprised the village in the night; and every one found in it—man, woman, and child—was shot. The dragoman told us a story of an Englishman who took up his abode here for some years, and kept himself very much to himself, living the life of the people of the place. No one knew who he was, or whence he came. When a dahabeah or a felucca anchored near the shore, he never approached it, but retired to the hills, or remained within his house. The mysterious stranger disappeared as suddenly as he appeared, and "the place that knew him, knew him no more." To reach the caves, we got off the donkeys, and walked among rocks and boulders, and through the sand up to the steep hill rising above the rich valley which stretches along the river. In the tomb of Knum-Hotef there is the fresco of a procession of shepherds, headed by a man leading a wild goat as a present to the king, and also some water-fowl; while, looking out from the panniers of one ass, are seen the heads of two children, and in the panniers of another, some jars of stibium. A man, painted of a red colour, and who carries an ibis, closes the procession. It was at one time supposed by some that in this procession they discovered the coming down into Egypt of Jacob and his sons. Could this have been proved, it would have given a tenfold interest to the fresco ; but the opinion has been now satisfactorily refuted ; and as the tomb bears date in the reign of Osirtasen I., it must have been hewn out and closed up many centuries before Joseph was sold into Egypt. The features of the men, their black beards, and dress, however, and the character of the whole procession, give colour to the idea that they are a foreign family coming to settle in Egypt, very much after the manner of Jacob and his sons when they migrated from Canaan to the land of the Pharaohs. The tomb of Ameni-Amenemha is also interesting from its frescoes, and vaulted roof, which is richly starred ; and from the lotus pillars which spring from a circular base, and which are bound together just below the capital, which is formed of four lobes of these beautiful water-plants. Every one will note the Christian symbols that occur in these and in the other rock-tombs of Egypt, for they were used by the anchorites in the early Christian centuries as their abodes, and they have left traces of themselves upon the walls. Here you see the cross, with doves resting upon it, representing Christ in His sacrifice, and the Holy Spirit in His grace ; here, too, you see the trefoil, which is a type of the Trinity, and the letters Alpha and Omega are so connected with it that they form the monogram of

Christ with which we are all familiar. It may have been owing to the fanaticism of the Christian monks that the plaster on which the hieroglyphics are painted has been broken, and the figures defaced; and though we can understand their abhorrence of idolatry, yet we cannot but mourn that at Beni-Hassan and elsewhere so much has been destroyed that would have thrown light on the history of the times.

That evening the boat was moored at Beni-Hassan, and early the next morning, Friday, January 6th, we proceeded up the Nile, passing the steep mountain range called Gebel-abou-Fedah, which rises abruptly from the river, just before reaching the large town of Manfalout.

We learn from Mariette that high up in these mountains are the famous grottos of Maabdeh, to which access is obtained through a natural fissure in the rock, and which are literally filled with mummies of crocodiles, intermingled with some human mummies, the richest of which are gilded from head to foot, whilst even the poorest can boast of some decoration in the form of square-shaped leaves of gold, placed in immediate contact with the skin.

At Assiout, the capital of Upper Egypt, a town 250 miles from Cairo, we anchored for the night. The banks of the Nile from Cairo to Assiout are

flat.   The scenery lacks beauty, and many might call
the passage as far as this monotonous.   But although
there is no grandeur about the Nile up to this point,
or indeed still farther up the river, there is a great
deal of variety, and the monotony is sweet, and calm,
and dreamy.   On either bank a rich green spreads for
some distance, and the plain is dotted with Arab
villages ; the brown of the mud of which they are
built looks golden in the sunlight ; while here rises a
grove of graceful palms, and yonder is a mosque with
its rounded cupola and slender minaret.   The scene
is enlivened by groups of Arabs, with their asses and
camels laden with their different burdens, or by a bevy
of women, with their jars poised gracefully on their
heads, and coming down to the river for water.   Every
village has not only its mosque, but its dovecote, and
hundreds of pigeons wing their way through the
bright and cloudless sky.   Yonder is a shadoof, with
its droning, melancholy noise, worked by men ; and
yonder a sakieh, turned by the labour of a patient
buffalo or ox.   Then birds, new and strange to us,
engage the attention.   A group of pelicans upon some
pit of sand wait for their prey, and the so-called ibis,
or paddy-bird, white and solitary as a ghost, stands
on a jutting rock, or beside the bank ; the beautiful
black and white striped kingfisher hovers in the air,

and fans it with its wings, ready to dart upon some unwitting fish when it appears near the surface ; or the brown buzzard or mottled vulture sweeps through the sky ; or a hawk with outspread wings poises itself in the air. It was interesting, too, to watch the long string of wild geese, under the conduct of their leader, forming into graceful figures as they flew homeward in the sunset, and caught some of its glory on their wings. And the sunsets—how beautiful they were ! and how brilliant the after-glow!

No! I cannot call the Nile monotonous ; and if there be something of sameness in the landscape, yet there is an endless variety in the aspect of the country ; and there are so many opportunities of going ashore, and visiting the temples, the tombs, the rock-caves, and the villages, that there is little or no reason to complain of monotony. If you feel somewhat wearied with the tameness of the scenery, then you have only to turn to your books, or to the pleasant people you are sure of meeting on board the steamer. Very agreeable was the party on board the *Rameses*, many of them hailing from across the Atlantic, some from the Far West. Amongst these was a former governor of Michigan, with his wife and daughters—a man who has won golden opinions in his own country, from the interest he takes in every

G

religious and philanthropic object. Another gentleman from America was an artist of great ability, and
his sketches were something beautiful. He and his
handsome wife added much to the pleasure of their
fellow-passengers. We had on board an Irish noble-
man, with his wife and daughters, and an English
viscount. Also the uncle of an English peer, an in-
defatigable chess-player, who too often, though not
always, came off victorious. We had also on board an
enthusiastic angler from Monmouthshire, who, though
with a lively and intelligent interest in all that he saw,
evidently preferred the Usk to the Nile, and looked
forward with a pleasurable anticipation to the time
when, with rod in hand, he would be able to pursue
his favourite sport. His wife sketched admirably, and
also took the greatest pleasure in our visits to colossal
temples and ancient tombs. The other gentlemen
and ladies on board, whether married or single,
contributed to make the passage up the Nile very
pleasant ; and what with reading, writing, conversation, chess, and visits to places of historical interest,
the hours passed most agreeably away.

For those who have time to spare, and money to
spend, a dahabeah must be the pleasantest and most
satisfactory way of visiting the Nile, for this gives
you the opportunity of seeing the wonderful temples

of the land at your leisure, and you are not hurried over places where you desire to linger. You may stop for a day or days, just as suits your wishes. Yet a dahabeah has its disadvantages, and you may, from want of a favourable wind, have to " tie up " at some spot entirely devoid of interest, and be detained there for days against your will. Or you may have to " track " at a slow pace, and be compelled to pity the poor men who in the heat of the day have to drag your boat along.

Perhaps a steam dahabeah is on the whole the most desirable way of going up the Nile, when not only the strong current of the river is against you, but when a high wind may blow from the south. And though it is said that the prevalent wind in Egypt is from the north, I must say that my experience of the wind in January was that it blew almost always from the south, and that most disagreeably. It was cold, too, so cold that I have been glad to put on both an over-coat and an Inverness cape, and sometimes it brought the sand in clouds, filling the air with a misty haze. At first the climate disappointed me. I had expected to find warm days and balmy air, and I was told that the weather was "a constant," so invariably fine that it never was made a subject of conversation as in England. But so far from " one day telling another,"

there were continual changes; and after our first morning's greeting as we came on deck with the other
passengers, the usual remark was, " How cold it is ! "
or, " There is a prospect of finer weather to-day;" or,
" I hope it will be warmer than yesterday." But
though it was cold, the air was dry and exhilarating ;
and skies that looked dim and cloudy, and which in
England would have portended a wet day, never dis-
charged themselves in rain, and became bright and
blue after a few hours. As far as my experience goes,
I do not think that Egypt is a climate for those who
are seriously ill, for these great and sudden changes of
temperature, and the quantity of fine sand or dust
that is borne along by some winds, must be prejudicial
to all with pulmonary diseases ; but if you are fairly
well, and wish to escape the rigours of an English
winter or spring, I should think no country could be
better. Invalids whose health is in a precarious state,
or who require comforts, must find Egypt in many respects very trying. The meat, except perhaps in the
best Cairo hotels, is hard and indigestible, and I have
sometimes been obliged to send away my plate with
the beef or mutton or fowl hardly touched. And no
doubt this arises from the necessity of cooking the
meat soon after it is killed. The sheep you saw yesterday happily nibbling the grass, is served up in slices

to-day as the *pièce de résistance ;* and the fowl that this morning was brought to the boat or the hotel with its wings tied together behind its back, you eat with your salad before the pudding. The invalid's appetite is generally both delicate and fastidious, and requires coaxing, and there is nothing to coax it in the hotels or on the Nile steamers, comfortable as they are, and consequently the invalid suffers. I have heard more than once loud complaints on this head.

CHAPTER IX.

A SSIOUT is the capital of Upper Egypt, and here the Governor of Upper Egypt resides. His palace stands among acacias and palms, and the mimosa, with its bright yellow flowers, which contrast well with the dark foliage of the trees. The town is well situated, and contains some fine, well-built houses. As we passed through the streets, we found the market thronged with camels, and buffaloes, and donkeys, laden with the produce of the district ; and here men from the country in their long cloaks, and veiled women in blue robes, were busy making their purchases. There was once a large slave market here, but this, happily, is abolished, and we may hope for ever. The bazaars are very good, and knives and swords and battle-axes may be bought, also articles of pretty brown pottery, with fly-brushes, and ivory, richly embroidered saddles, and ornaments in silver and gold.

A short ride beyond Assiout, the Lycopolis of the Greeks, where the wolf was worshipped, are tombs cut in the rock, where the mummies of the sacred animal were deposited. Mummied wolves have been found in the caves in the mountain, and also mummied jackals. One of these is to be seen in the Egyptian Room at the British Museum. The tombs are of very ancient date. There is one cave called "Stabl d'Antar"—the stable of Antar—which is spacious and lofty, the ceiling being covered with patterns in blue and grey, and the hieroglyphic sculptures coloured in red and blue. At the entrance of some of the caves were fragments of human bones and bits of mummy cloth, and the Arabs who followed us up the hill offered these for sale.

That which pleased me most was the fine view from the hills to Assiout, with its mosques and minarets, and over the Nile Valley to the river, which wound like a thread of silver through the plain, green with the young corn, interspersed with the graceful palm. To the east is the purple outline of the Arabian hills; and to the west, as we turn round on the brow of the rock of Djebil, we see the golden light and soft violet shadows that fall on the distant desert sands.

And all this seen through a luminous atmosphere. It is a prospect to charm the eye, and we lingered as long as we could to enjoy a landscape of such beauty.

In the caves of the Djebil, Christian hermits took up their residence, as in many other caves along the Nile ; and from them may have sprung the legend that Joseph and Mary made their dwelling here when they brought the young Child down into Egypt at the command of God. It is not likely, however, that the holy family journeyed so far, and most probably either Memphis or Heliopolis was the place which they made their home.

Assiout is 294 miles from Cairo. The boat anchored for the night at Maghaga, and early on the morning of Sunday was again on her way south. Divine service was held on board in the large saloon ; and pleasant it was to join in spirit with friends at home in the beautiful words of our Liturgy, and to lift with them our voices in prayer and praise to Him who has promised to be present with the two or three who are met together in His name.

Tahtah, Sohag, and Girgheh, once the capital of Middle Egypt, were passed, and also Bellianeh, the town from which Abydos is visited, and we sailed by it reluctantly, but with the hope that we should see the celebrated temple on our return journey down the river. The scenery was now for the most part picturesque, the distant range of the Libyan hills being seen to the east ; and to the west, on the Arabian side of the Nile, the line of hills came down near the river. The rocks on the western bank were of limestone, and were honeycombed with tombs. Palmgroves and villages were left behind ; and mud huts, each with its pierced parapet for pigeons and doves. And here the fertile land was narrowed to a very small strip of green between the cliffs and the river. It was cold still, and a strong gale from the south made overcoats and wraps a continued necessity, and drew from us many exclamations of surprise. At sunset the wind generally fell, though the evenings and nights were very chilly, and we were glad to have the deck of the steamer closed in with an awning, which gave it the protection and the comfort of a room. But we were only in the beginning of January, and the air was uniformly dry ; there was no rain ; and when we landed to ride on donkeys to some temple or tomb, and the mid-day sun came out, we often found it hot enough.

The dragoman called our attention to a Moslem tomb on the eastern bank of the river, and informed us that here Sheykh Seleem was buried. Who was

Sheykh Seleem? He was a Mohammedan saint, who lived for years on the banks of the Nile, never wore even a strip of clothing, never washed himself, never moved from the spot on which he sat, through the heats of summer or the colds of winter, and never did anything to procure himself food or water. It is said that he did not even feed himself, and that meat and drink were put into his mouth by the hands of those who came to see, and to get the blessing of the saint. He grew enormously fat, and throve upon his indolence and beggary. He was considered very holy, his holiness being in exact proportion to his dirtiness; he died at a good old age in the very odour of sanctity, and his tomb is regarded as an object of the deepest veneration.

On Monday, January 9th, the steamer stopped on the left bank of the river, opposite Kenneh, and donkeys were in readiness to take us to the temple of Denderah, a ride of about half an hour. There was the usual crowd of men and boys with their donkeys on the shore; the usual cries of "This very good donkey, sir;" "This Telegraph;" "This Flying Dutchman;" "His very bad donkey, this better;" and the usual struggle to get one's self free, and choose the animal which we thought best. The dragoman had often to be appealed to, to rescue us from the importunities with which we were beset ; and I must say that these scenes on shore—the conflicts—for they are nothing short of this—are most disgraceful and ought to be put an end to, if possible.

CHAPTER X.

THE beautiful temple of Denderah is dedicated to
Hathor, the Egyptian Venus, and the nurse of
Horus, son of Osiris and Isis, and is comparatively
modern, belonging to the period of the Ptolemies and
the Cæsars. Every temple or tomb in Egypt that
does not date from three or four thousand years
before Christ is considered modern, and therefore is
not stamped with that seal of antiquity which in the
eyes of many gives a value to a building beyond any
other. Antiquity has its interest, but so has beauty ;
and the works of the Ptolemies and the Cæsars are
not to be passed by with a sneer because comparatively new. The temple of Denderah was begun by
Cleopatra, and not finished till the reign of Nero.
Belzoni extols it as the most magnificent he had seen,

and says that he was more impressed by it than by any other. It is indeed a magnificent temple, with a grand portico, and the walls are covered with innumerable inscriptions and bas-reliefs, and an infinite number of sculptured figures. The great hall has twenty-four columns of great size, crowned with heads of Isis, and adorned with carvings and hieroglyphics. Every wall and pillar and frieze has its own special adornment, worked out in the most minute detail; while on the architrave above are processions of priests and warriors, kings and gods, sculptured in the most delicate and beautiful manner. On the ceiling of the portico is a painting of the famous zodiac of the age of Augustus, and there are several chapels, or sanctuaries, for the use of the king and the priests, for festivals and processions, and for shrines to receive the images of the gods. In the old Egyptian religion there appears to be no place for the people; "they were rigidly excluded from the temples and their precincts, and seem to have been allowed no participation in the worship of the gods." None but those of royal or priestly birth were admitted to the solemn ceremonies. These were considered too sacred for the common people, and for them the religious services of the temple were veiled in mystery. In the stately processions that marched through these

cloisters and corridors they never took any part ;
from the worship offered to these strange deities with
the heads of the hawk, or the ibis, or the cow, they
were excluded ; not for them the mystic ceremonies
conducted beneath these Hathor-headed columns,
and architraves with paintings of the sacred scarabeii,
and filled with hieroglyphic inscriptions ; the kings
and the priests alone had the privilege of paying
adoration to the gods in the sanctuary where the
divine images were placed.

On the outside walls of the temple are figures of
the celebrated queen, Cleopatra, and her son by Julius
Cæsar, the young Cæsareon.   It was interesting to
look upon a portrait of the famous woman who led
kings captive by her fascination, " whose charms age
could not wither, custom could not stale "; but her
beauty is of a sensual and voluptuous character, and
more of the Oriental than the Western type.   The
features are fat and full.   On her head she wears the
horned disc of Hathor, the vulture of the goddess
Maut, and the horns of Isis; and her hair, falling below
the head-dress, is arranged in a number of small plaits,
not very unlike what may be seen on the head of
a Nubian belle.   Very good photographs may be
obtained of this portrait of the Egyptian queen, and
there are also reliefs in plaster of Paris, in which the

face is coloured in yellow, the ground of the tableau being blue. A great part of the temple is in ruins, and the havoc wrought on the pylon and the sacred places is no doubt the work of the early Christians, who, in their iconoclastic zeal, mutilated this and other sacred places which, but for their iconoclasm, might have remained perfect to the present day. While we acknowledge their zeal for God, we cannot but mourn over its result. The wild bees, too, have done much mischief to the carvings and sculptures on the walls. They have covered the hieroglyphics and figures with innumerable mud cells. These destructive bees are larger than our hive bees, and are very pretty insects; their head and breast is of an orange colour, and the abdomen is of a glossy black. They have destroyed much of the decorative work on the temple walls. You ascend by a richly sculptured staircase on the northern side, on which is seen a procession of priests, with the king at their head, to the terraced roof, from whence you obtain a fine view of the valley, and the distant hills glowing in the sunlight, and where the shadows fall, taking all tender tints of violet, and rose, and blue. The plain between you and the hill is green with lentils and springing corn, and bean fields, through which the river, like a thread of silver, takes its fertilizing and beneficent course.

Leaving the terrace with reluctance, and with one more look at the temple, we again mount our donkeys, and return to the boat. That evening, as we steam to Luxor, we see the great temple of Karnak in the distance, and presently the grand ruined temple of Luxor lines the shore, and the good ship *Rameses* is to anchor here till Friday. The three days during which the large steamers remain here give the passengers the opportunity of seeing the Theban Valley, with its temples and tombs, the two magnificent Colossi, as well as the temples of Luxor and Karnak ; but three days is but a short time for all these wonderful monuments of Egypt's ancient glory; and I was glad to take up my quarters at the Luxor Hotel for a month, after coming back from Wady Halfa. This month gave me full opportunity of visiting the valley of the Tombs of the Kings, and some of the grandest ruins in the world ; and I made as much use as possible of the weeks spent there to inspect scenes so deservedly famous. I shall therefore at once mention the impression they made on me, and refer to the life at Luxor when I speak of my return to the place from the Nubian frontier.

The city of Thebes was built on both sides of the Nile, just as London is built on both sides of the Thames, or Paris on both sides of the Seine.

"Thebes," as Mr. Reginald Stuart Poole tells us in his *Cities and Monuments of Egypt,* "had, like the other cities of Egypt, a civil and a religious name. The civil name was Apiu, 'the city of thrones,' which, with the article 't,' or 'ta,' became Ta-Apiu, and was identified by the Greeks with the name of their once famous city, by us corruptly called Thebes. The sacred name was Nu-Amen, 'the city of Amen,' the god of Thebes; or simply Nu, 'the city,' and Nu-ā, 'the great city.' In these names we recognise the No-Amon, and No of Scripture." Ammon-Ra, typified by the sun, is the principal deity worshipped at Thebes, and with him is associated Maut, the divine mother, and Chonsu, the offspring of both—they form the Theban trinity.

Thebes must have been a large and magnificent city, with its palaces and temples, its hundred gates, its public buildings, and its private dwellings. Of the city there is no trace. All that remains of its grandeur are the two temples of Luxor and Karnak on the eastern shore, and the temples of El Goornah, the Rameseum, and Medinet-Habou, on the western shore. Luxor is a small market town of some m-portance, the residence of the English, the American, and the Italian consuls. There are now two hotels, the Luxor and the Karnak, and many visitors of all nations reside there for some months in the winter. The town is a cluster of mud houses, and many of these are grouped, to its disfigurement, round the ruins of the temple. The English consul had his house between the temple pillars, but happily another is being built for him, which no doubt he now occupies. Luxor has for its background the Arabian hills, while the Libyan hills, with the Theban plain, and the two sitting Colossi, are immediately in front; and beyond these, and hidden by the yellow hills, are the Tombs of the Kings. The two towers of the propylon of the temple at Luxor are situated towards the north, and face towards Karnak, which is about two miles off, and a solitary obelisk of red granite rises close by. The companion obelisk is now in the Place de la Concorde, at Paris. It is supposed that a dromos, or avenue of 1,200 krios-headed sphinxes, led from the entrance of this temple to the grand propylon at Karnak; and many of these sphinxes, now mutilated and broken, may be seen near the latter, and they give an idea of the glory of the structure when kings and priests moved in solemn procession to the shrine of God. The temple at Luxor was founded by Amenophis III., who built the portico, the courts, the hall of assembly, and the sanctuary; but Rameses II. constructed a stately approach to its walls, and commemorated his victories on them, and raised statues of himself, as was his custom. Two of these are broken and disfigured, but there is one standing erect farther to the south, the face of which is perfect ; and just beneath, in a recess covered by a stone which is easily removed, is a female head, said to be that of his wife. On the towers are sculptures of Rameses in his chariot, attended by his army, and waging war against the enemy ; now he is depicted as drawing his bow, now he is victorious over the foe, and now he is returning in state from the battle-field. The temple of Luxor shows signs of additions made by kings of later dynasties. For amongst the cartouches found on the walls of the sanctuary are those of Ptolemy Philopater, and of Alexander the younger, also of Amentounkh, and of Psammetichus. Besides battle scenes, there are sculptured on the ruins figures of the gods ; and here the Theban triad appear— Ammon-Ra, Maut, and their son Chonsu. These are the deities that preside over the various scenes that are enacted.

The temple of Luxor is overshadowed by the splendours of the temple of Karnak. The distance from Luxor to Karnak is two miles.

The road to Karnak skirts the village, and lies

through fields of lentils and corn, with here and there a group of palms and sycamores which throw a grateful shade over the ground. The Nile lies low, and out of sight. To the east rise the Arabian hills, glowing and golden in the sunlight. Presently are seen in front the two pylons and portal, the towering walls and pillars of the great temple. Two obelisks of red granite also meet your wondering gaze,—the one to the east the tallest in Egypt—the tallest in the world. This is a monolith, 108 feet high, the work of Queen Hatasou, and once covered with a coating of gold. There is a fallen one which was also gilded, the work of the same queen, and both obelisks had an apex of pure gold. From an inscription on the pedestal, we learn that these two obelisks were hewn out of the quarry, were put up and sculptured in the incredibly short space of seven months.[1] The name of the artist who conceived and executed this magnificent monument was Semnut I. I find it difficult to describe the magnificent temple of Karnak, with its avenue of broken sphinxes—some andros-headed, some krios-headed; its great hall, with its 134 gigantic columns ; its beautiful lotus and papyrus pillars ; its walls open to the sky, and sculptured with gods

---

[1] Mariette says " nineteen months."

and kings, and processions of priests; and its clerestory, through whose bars you catch glimpses of the cloudless blue. The twelve colossal central columns (I give the measurement as recorded by Miss Edwards) are 62 feet high in the shaft (or about seventy with the plinth and abacus), and measure 34 feet 6 inches in circumference. "All are buried to a depth of between six and seven feet in the alluvial deposits of between three and four thousand annual inundations." The noble hypæthral hall fills us with awe as we stand and look around, and think of the mighty dead who conceived and executed buildings of such majesty and beauty. Truly, "there were giants in those days." "The imagination which in Europe," says Champollion, "rises far above our porticos, sinks abashed at the foot of the one hundred and forty columns of the hypostyle hall at Karnak." And no wonder, for the area of this hall is 57,629 feet in size, and from the measurements above given of the columns they will be seen to be proportionately high. As I stood in the central hall, in the midst of a forest of shafts and stupendous pillars —one enormous column moved from its place, and caught in its fall on the top of another—I thought nothing could be more beautiful or impressive than the view to the east. There, standing beyond the temple, rose a single palm against the sky; and far away in the distance were the wild Libyan hills. And this little glimpse of nature among the works of man, independently of its own beauty, came upon the eye with a soothing effect ; if man's work crushed you with a sense of your own insignificance, God's work reminded you of One " whose tender mercies are over all His works," who cares for the lily of the field, and without whom not a sparrow falleth to the ground.

There is a beautiful sanctuary in the temple, filled with sculptures and hieroglyphs, and where the colour is marvellously brilliant and fresh — more especially the reds and blues. It is worth spending some time in it, and looking carefully over the great variety of detail. It will repay minute and repeated inspection. There are roofless chambers, fallen statues, shattered columns, and a mutilated Colossus of Rameses II. Indeed, Karnak is but a vast collection of magnificent ruins. The temple is supposed to have been planned by Amenophis III., who also founded the temple at Luxor, and who erected in the Theban plain the two sitting Colossi, which are statues of himself. The hypostyle hall was begun by Seti I., the father of Rameses II., and was finished by the latter monarch, whose colossal statues are everywhere, and who glorified himself, as though he were a god. It is said that the overthrow of this incomparable temple was due to an earthquake ; and that Cambyses, the fierce and fanatical Persian, and Ptolemy Lathyrus only completed the destruction which had been begun by some terrible convulsion of nature. Whatever was the cause, the temple, with its famous hypostyle hall, which Fergusson calls "the greatest of man's architectural works," is now but a majestic ruin. It was once, as Dean Stanley says, "the grandest building which the world ever raised to the glory and worship of God.'" He also speaks of it as "the oldest consecrated place of worship in the world," and says, "the principles of religious art first appeared here, and have never since been lost." On the southern wall, beyond the Osiride figure, mutilated and maimed—beyond the sanctuary, there is a sculpture of the greatest interest, and which has a reference to Bible history. Shishank—the Shishak of the Bible—and one of the last of the Pharaohs, who for more than a thousand years had assisted in building Karnak, like other great conquerors, left cut in the stone a record of his conquests. There you see him leading captive the representatives of more than thirty nations whom he had subdued, and the name of each is written in hieroglyphics on a cartouche.

He holds by the hair a group of captives, distinctly
Jewish in feature, and Judah is mentioned among the
vanquished nations. We turn to the sacred history, and
light is thrown on the sculptures at once. In the 1st
Book of Kings, 14th chapter and 25th verse, we read :
" In the fifth year of King Rehoboam, Shishak, king
of Egypt, came up against Jerusalem." We have
the same record in 2 Chronicles xii. 39. On the
wall on which this interesting sculpture is seen, but
some way to the east, we see cut into the stone the
celebrated poem of Pentaour, a poet at the court of
Rameses II.

Having examined these interesting records of a
remote period, we rode through a mass of broken
columns and mounds of brick, past a little lake, fed
by the Nile through the soil which is charged with
saltpetre, and the waters of which are salt and unfit for
use, and came to the long avenue of broken sphinxes,
some of them with human heads, others with the
head of a ram, and which once extended to the banks
of the Nile. We then visited the ruins of the temple
of Maut, the divine mother, and rode back through
the fields, and by the houses that fringe the village,
to the hotel.

SUNSET ON THE NILE.

The sun in setting smites that river old,
  Which rolls through Egypt with life-giving flow;
  At once the placid waters gleam and glow,
And glisten like a sheet of burnished gold,
Bright as the sands o'er which Pactolus rolled,
  In the far-distant ages long ago ;
But as I gaze, the splendour fades, and lo !
I wake to find the world grown dark and cold.

Yet now the night draws on with moon and star
  That fill with liquid light the purple skies ;
And Venus burns in beauty from afar,
And Sirius leans out from his silver car,
  While Mars looks down with red and fiery eyes,
As though he'd gird himself afresh for war.

CHAPTER XI.

THE morning was one of great expectation, and
no little excitement, on which we made our
arrangements to visit the plain of Thebes, on the
western banks of the Nile, and the bright and cloudless
dawn gave promise of a fine day. We were rowed
across the river in a small boat by some swarthy and
turbaned Arabs, who kept time to the stroke of their
oars with their usual song: " Hay-a-lee-sah! Hay-a-
lee-sah !" the song being a sort of monotonous chant.
When I asked the meaning of the words, I was told
that " Hala-ee-sah" was one of Noah's daughters,
and that the sailors were invoking her protection.
Whether this be the true meaning of the invocation,
I am unable to say. Sometimes the song would
take another form, and I believe the words were not
unseldom impromptu. When we reached the western

shore, there was the usual crowd of men and boys
with their donkeys, and the usual struggle to induce
you to take their beast, which was better than all the
others ; and the jostling and the crowding, the noise
and the excitement, was simply intolerable. Such
disgraceful scenes, so close to several Consulates and
a station of police, ought not to be permitted. It
was only by appeals to the dragoman, who could not
attend to all the party at once, and the indiscriminate
use of the stick, that deliverance from unseemly importunities could be effected. These Arabs, many of
them at least, are dishonest, and the jostling and
crowding give them an opportunity of putting their
hands into your pockets when off your guard. I lost a
purse in this way, and a friend of mine had his silver
cigar-case stolen. The whole scene is a disgrace, and
ought, by some means or other, to be stopped. The
donkeys were good; but care should be taken to see
that the saddles are properly girthed before mounting,
as more than once I have known them to slip on one
side, and the rider suddenly find himself prostrate
on the ground. Fortunately the Theban plain is of
deep sand, and the fall there is therefore not so serious
as it might otherwise be. But I have seen falls on the
hard road and among stones, and the consequence was
severe cuts and bruises on the head and face. Here, at

Thebes, besides your donkey-boy, you may be accompanied, if you like it, by a little girl clad in blue, adorned with a necklace of beads, earrings and bracelets, and sometimes a nose-ring, carrying a water-jar on her head, from which she will supply you at luncheon among the temples and tombs, for a small backsheesh. She will run beside your donkey for miles, and never seem tired; and if you will drink from her jar, of the same shape as you see sculptured on the temple walls, will reward you with a sweet smile from her coral lips. And what teeth she and all the people have! I never saw teeth so regular and so white. They are like a string of orient pearls; and it is a pleasure when the lips part, and you see them gleaming white as the driven snow.

After a ride across the sands, if it is early in the year, before the Nile has fallen much, you have to cross a channel of the river in a boat, and the donkeys also are put on board, some of them being very unwilling to be embarked, and sticks being plentifully used to get them to move. The Arabs are not tender to their beasts: they beat and use them cruelly, as the marks upon head and ears too surely prove. On reaching the other bank you have another short ride, and then another channel to cross; and then again you mount your donkeys, and riding down one steep bank, and up a second, you find yourself on the wonderful plain where the Colossi sit, and the temples stand, and from which lies the wild and rocky road to the Tombs of the Kings. If it is later in the year —February or March—the Nile is so low that the channels are dried up, and the need of all boats, save the first from Luxor, is gone.

As you ride on, you pass richly cultivated fields of wheat, and barley, and lentils, and maize, and you see many a sakieh and shadoof, and everywhere where the water winds is greenness and beauty.

Suppose we visit first the Tombs of the Kings, and enter the narrow defile which leads from El Goornah through the weird valley of Bab-el-Molouk. On each side of the valley, which forms a fitting entrance to the city of the dead, rise steep and barren limestone cliffs, of a bright yellow colour—broken, jagged, fantastic—which shut in the view, and hem you closely in on either side. Above is a burning sky; below are sands and loose stones, and masses of rock; and the whole scene is wild and desolate in the extreme. Not a blade of grass is to be seen. The sun scorches you from above: the heat is great; you long for a breath of cool air. You are shut in between limestone walls. You feel it to be a fitting approach to the valley of death beyond. At length the defile opens to a greater width, and you find

yourself in front of a mountain tapering up like a
pyramid, whose sides are perforated with tombs
which extend into the heart of the hills to the length
of some three or four hundred feet.   In visiting a
tomb, you pass through an entrance which slopes
downward into the heart of the mountain.   You enter
chamber after chamber, some of them supported by
pillars ; and on the walls of each are sculptures and
hieroglyphics appropriate to a place so solemn.   The
roofs of these tombs are lined with brick, and plastered
with stucco for the reception of the hieroglyphics ;
and over the portals there is a painting of the sun's
disc, the setting of this orb and his rising again being
regarded by the old Egyptians as a symbol of death
and resurrection.   For the same reason you see at
the entrance the figure of the crocodile, the emblem of
darkness, and the scarab, the emblem of resurrection,
portrayed, showing the belief of this people in a life beyond the grave.   These tombs, begun by the kings early
in life, and carried on through a long course of years,
were considered as "homes" of the dead.   At death
a new and still more important life was begun, and
they prepared their eternal habitations accordingly.

It is only since the year 1881 that any knowledge
has been obtained of the conceptions of the ancient
Egyptians as to the destiny of the soul, and the worship

of the dead. We learn from the inscriptions in the chambers where the sarcophagus was placed, that this chamber was considered the abode of the soul, the "Ba"; while the chapel at the entrance of the tomb was the abode of the spiritual body, the "Ka." This spiritual body was believed to be the faithful representation of the living person, and its home was in the chambers where the offerings were presented and the prescribed ceremonies were performed. The soul, often represented under the form of a heron, or by a hawk with a human head, was furnished with wings to enable it to fly to the other world, and to return to this. The "Ba" had chambers set apart for itself, near its body, now a mummy; and the "Ka" continued to make Egypt its home, and haunted the place where it used to reside while in its disembodied state. This "Ka," or spiritual body, was not regarded as immortal, for it was subject to a second death, or annihilation; and this death could be caused by the same means that caused the first death. The "Ka" was subject to the infirmities of the natural body; it was liable to hunger and thirst, and could be killed by the bite of venomous beasts. In the Ritual of the Dead are found prayers and supplications which are addressed to serpents and scorpions in order to avert their wrath, and to induce them not to injure the

"Ka." When the spiritual body moved abroad, and
was tortured by hunger or thirst, it had often to
feed on garbage in order to support life. To preserve
the "Ka" from death, offerings of fruit, and wine, and
meat, are represented on the chambers of the tombs.
The soul, which was also supposed to be mortal, had
similar offerings of food and drink, and selected from
them what it pleased. Both the "Ba" and the "Ka"
had a shade, which also subsisted on the table of
offerings, which was placed in the antechamber.
Sometimes the bread and wine, instead of being
given to the dead, were presented to the gods, who
from their own hands gave them to the mummy.
We learn from their conception of the "Ba" and the
"Ka," did we not learn it elsewhere, that the ancient
Egyptians distinctly recognised the immortality of
the soul and the resurrection of the body. We also
find from the Ritual of the Dead that they believed
in a judgment to come ; for not only is the judgment
of the soul seen in the sculptures on the walls of the
tombs, but in the rolls of papyrus found in the coffin
with the mummy, the course of the spirit after death
is traced to the world of recompense or retribution.
This we shall consider by-and-by. Let us wait no
longer outside the Tombs of the Kings, but enter, and
see their wonders.

The most important tombs are those marked No. 2, that of Rameses IV.; No. 6, Rameses IX.; No. 9, Rameses VI.; No. 11, Rameses III.; and No. 17, the tomb of Seti I., called "Belzoni's tomb," because discovered by Belzoni in 1816. The entrance to the tombs is by a sloping passage, at the end of which a long flight of steps leads down to a dark chamber, from which other dark chambers branch off, and the walls of which are covered with hieroglyphics, and with sculptures and paintings of the scenes through which the soul is to pass in its journey through Hades to Amenti. These corridors and chambers being in entire darkness, can only be inspected by the light of a candle carried in the hand, or by the stronger illumination of magnesium wire, which however gives a flash all too brief for our wishes, and then expires. How these paintings of serpents, scarabæi, and crocodiles, these representations of offerings of meat and libations of wine,—how these birds and beasts, these vases and ships, could ever have been drawn and coloured, considering the darkness of the tombs, is a marvel. What light had the sculptors and painters to work by? As they climbed to the top of the supporting walls, or to the ceilings above, whence did they procure the bright and steady light by which they were enabled to portray the signs of

I

the zodiac, to colour the vestments, and paint the
vases of silver and gold ? In many of the tombs
may be seen an empty sarcophagus, holding the position it did of old when placed there by loving hands
long since mouldering in the grave. But some of the
sarcophagi have been removed—shall we say by
profane hands?—and the sarcophagus of Seti I.,
which was brought to England by Belzoni, is now
in Sir John Soane's Museum ; and the sarcophagus
of Rameses III. is in the Fitzwilliam Museum at
Cambridge, the lid which covered it being in the
Egyptian hall of the Louvre. The most interesting
of the tombs are perhaps those of Seti I., with its
dark chambers and corridors, which are covered with
the wanderings of the disembodied spirit, and scenes
from the life to come ; and the tomb of Rameses III.,
known as "The Harper's tomb," from the figures of
two harpers clothed in white, on the walls, who sweep
the strings of their ten-stringed harps. On the
chambers of this tomb are pictured furniture and
arms, gardens and fishponds, birds and beasts ; servants kneading bread, some killing cattle for the feast,
others preparing it for the cook. In each of these
smaller chambers is a closed pit, which is supposed
by Sir G. Wilkinson to have been the burial-place of
that officer of the royal household, whether high

steward, treasurer, or chief butler, or baker, gardener, or armour-bearer, whose functions are illustrated on the walls. This tomb gives one a good idea of the luxury that prevailed in those old days, of the wealth and artistic taste of the Egyptian kings at the time when Israel was ruled by judges, and Deborah was urging Barak, the son of Abinoam, to battle against the Philistines.

We cannot look upon these splendid tombs of the royal dead without recalling the words of the prophet: " All the kings of the nations, even all of them, lie in glory, every one in his own house " (Isa. xiv. 18).

After leaving the tombs, with their mystery and gloom, it was pleasant to emerge into the glorious sunlight, climb up one of the steep ridges of the Libyan hills, and see the green plain stretching out underneath, and the blue Nile flowing between you and the Arabian chain, and the remains of temples and palaces in the level valley. Luxor and Karnak were in the distance ; and below you the Rameseum and Medinet-Habou, and the two Colossi keeping their silent watch over the whole. There, where are now only a few broken columns and ruined arches,—there, where lies some broken and defaced gigantic statue, once rose the noble city or the splendid palace ; and over yon mounds of sand rode the king in his chariot, attended by his great men, or followed by the captives whom he had conquered, and who graced his brilliant triumph. Imagination peoples the now lonely valley. The streets are thronged with multitudes passing to and fro, men and women who fill the haunts of business or of pleasure ; and in the shops there is "the merchandise of gold and silver and precious stones, and of pearls, and fine linen and purple, and silk, and scarlet, and all thyine wood, and all manner of vessels of ivory, and all kinds of most precious wood, and brass and iron and marble, and cinnamon, and odours, and ointments, and frankincense, and wine, and oil, and fine flour and wheat, and cattle, and sheep, and horses, and chariots and slaves." On the Nile are gay boats with brilliant pennons, and a long line of rowers ; and as the queen or some noble lady glides along the smooth waters, the scene is one of magnificence and beauty.

> "The barge she sat in, like a burnished throne,
> Burned on the water ; the poop was beaten gold,
> Purple the sails, and so perfumèd that
> The winds were love-sick with them ; the oars were silver,
> Which to the tune of lutes kept stroke."

You may sit on that Libyan hill and dream of the past, and call it up before you in a vision, and a sigh may escape you that all this glory has passed away; but as you think, you will soon feel grateful that a better, purer faith is now dominant among the civilized nations of the world, and that this will spread and increase even like the inundation of the once sacred river, until it touches and fertilizes every region of the globe.

CHAPTER XII.

IN the Theban plain there is a very interesting temple, at the entrance to the weird Bab-el-Molouk, "the valley of the kings," which I visited on several occasions. It is the temple of Goornah, and behind it is the cemetery called "Drah-Abou-Neggah." Built by Seti I., the temple was intended to be a monument to perpetuate the glory of his father, Rameses I. His greater son, Rameses II., completed the temple ; and as he raised monument after monument to his own glory, he intended that this also, in its extended form, should commemorate his fame.

On one of the doorways are the cartouches of Menephtah, the Pharaoh of the Exodus, the son of Rameses II., and his successor on the throne. But that which gives its especial interest to the temple of Goornah are the sculptured portraits of Rameses I., of

Seti I., and his queen Tua—the mother of Rameses II.—and the portrait of Rameses II. himself. These Pharaohs are all mild in aspect, and have handsome features. They bear a resemblance to the mummies in the Boulák Museum; the contour of the faces is the same, and there is the same delicacy in the lines of the profile. Rameses I. is represented as standing behind the gods, and crowned like Osiris; he is worshipped by his son, Seti I., and watches his grandson, Rameses II., as he pays homage to the gods, and pours a libation to the statue of his father. The great god, Ammon-Ra, presents the symbol of life to Rameses II., and the inscription on the temple wall runs thus: " Rameses, the beloved of Ammon, has dedicated this work to his father, Ammon-Ra, king of gods, having made additions for him to the temple of his father, the king, son of the sun, Osiris."

Some study should be given to the ruined pylon, and the portico with its ten columns which bear the likeness of the papyri, whose stalks, bound together below the capital, expand now, only to be gathered in again by the abacus. The fine sculptures demand examination : the various offerings to the gods, such as the vine with its bunches of grapes ; the boat with the ram's head ; the funeral car, shaped like a lion ; the asps on the cornices ; and the portal, whose ceiling is

adorned with cartouches and golden stars on an
azure ground.   I visited this beautiful temple several
times, and always with fresh admiration.   Familiarity
with its columns and porticoes, and with the history
of the august dead portrayed on its walls, always
gave it a new and increasing interest.

The man who provided my party with donkeys, and
the indispensable pendant of each—a donkey-boy—
was a fine, handsome man, tall, well made, with a small
moustache and beard, and a clear bronze complexion.
The Arab dress, with its graceful folds, became him
well, and set off his tall, slender figure to advantage.
His eyes were dark and piercing, and a row of beautifully white and regular teeth gleamed from his full and
red lips.   He lives on the western side of the Nile,
close to the temple of El Goornah.   He is a man well-
to-do, having a small farm, two camels, and two or
three cows.   He has two wives, and he and his two
brothers live near one another, in a sort of compound,
and seem to have a joint interest in the donkeys,
which were good, strong, sure-footed beasts.   He was
most anxious that I should go and see his house, and
his wives and children.   This I promised to do ; I much
wished to see the interior of a Fellah's home.   So as
his house was near El Goornah, I went there on one
of my visits to the temple.   Aboo-Neo was not at

home himself, but his wives were expecting me, and also his eldest brother's family, so that my party had a welcome from the women, who came to meet us, and to invite us into their cottage. Cottage it could hardly be called, for it was more of a mud hut, dark, and dusty, and stifling, and a place where one would think no human being could live. Beyond the first room was a second, to which ingress could only be had through a hole in the wall, closed by a door, and which had no window, or means of natural light, so that it was needful to carry a candle with you, if you were to see around you at all. It was a place more for cattle to herd than men to live in ; and indeed the cattle and the fowls seemed to make it their home, and to dwell familiarly with the human tenants. Aboo-Neo's wives were not so handsome as their husband, and looked older ; but women in the East soon lose their beauty and their youthful appearance, and grow prematurely old. The young girls who used to follow us with their water-jars gracefully poised on their heads, were generally very pretty agile and light, with dark eyes and hair, and a pleasant smile which showed their glittering teeth ; but destined as they were to be married at thirteen or fourteen, they would soon become worn-looking, wrinkled women, their grace and their beauty gone

for ever. The household of my donkey provider was
stirred at our coming—wives, children, and a little
baby, which one of the women carried in her arms,
came out to meet us. Coffee was prepared, and was
handed to us hot and smoking—the usual sweet
coffee without milk, and which, when the little cup
is emptied, leaves thick grounds at the bottom. We
drank it with many thanks, and, as the sun had great
power, we sat outside the house under the shadow of
a tree, and talked as well as we could with our hospit-
able friends. Our Arabic did not carry us very far ;
but the few sentences we knew, and the knowledge
gained under a teacher, were of some use. One of
the women brought out some antiques found among
the temples, and some blue beads, and a small brown
jar, and gave them to my daughters ; and the mother
of the baby took a necklace containing some charms
off her infant's neck, and would have given them like-
wise, but this we refused to accept, as the sacrifice
would have been far too great, and so we restored
it to the smiling child. We then shook hands with
the women, and bade them good-bye, pleased to see
the interior of an Arab's dwelling, but leaving it
with a feeling of wonder that it was possible for any
one to live and thrive in such houses, more wretched
than any I have ever seen in any country where

I have travelled, with the exception of Palestine, where they are of a similar character, quite as dark, stifling, and dirty.

THE THEBAN PLAIN.

The moon lights up the city of the dead,
  The temples and the tombs of mighty kings,
  And o'er the Libyan hills her lustre flings,
While on a kingdom's dust I lonely tread.
Here hearts rejoiced, or, wounded, inly bled,
  Sick of the hope deferred, the grief that brings
  Grey hairs—the cruel jealousy that stings—
The passionate love that yearns, and dies unfed.

"Oh, where are they," I said, "who lived and died ?
  Who wept or smiled, or knew the joys of fame ? "
A cloud pass'd o'er the moon,—the faint wind sighed,
  The pale stars shivered, hid their lambent flame,
And in my ears a ghostly voice replied,
  "The greatest are but shadows, or—a name ! "

CHAPTER XIII.

THE Rameseum is a wonderful ruin, with lines of pillars and ranges of courts and chambers. It contains a hall one hundred feet in length, with lotus columns, supporting roofs of a beautiful blue, and studded with yellow stars. The ruin is a very grand one, and the ground is strewn with huge fragments of wall, fallen columns, and broken pillars. The glory must have been very great when this magnificent structure stood in all its original splendour, a palace as well as a temple—the palace of Rameses II., and the temple of Ammon-Ra. Here, amongst the other ruins, lies the colossal but shattered statue of the great king. It is of beautiful red granite, highly polished, and is the largest statue that has been found in Egypt, by some inches larger than the statues of the two Colossi, the warders of the plain. More than one cartouche is deeply engraven on the hard red stone. You can climb up the huge mass, and view the temple and the scene around you from this elevated position. The features are destroyed, it is said by the Arabs, who hewed millstones out of the face. Sir G. Wilkinson, in his *Modern Egypt and Thebes*, says that its weight is about 887 tons 5½ cwt. The breadth between the shoulders is 22 feet 4 inches, and it must have stood some 60 feet high. The measure of the foot is nearly 11 feet in length, and 4 feet 10 inches in breadth. The mystery remains how such an enormous mass of granite could have been transported from the quarries of Syene, some hundred of miles away. How it was raised, how it was overthrown,—whether by the hand of violence, or, as some travellers suppose, by an earthquake,—is still a matter of conjecture; and why that mighty statue fell will never be known. The sculptures on the walls of the temple, on the great hall, and the various chambers, are similar to those met with elsewhere. Indeed, there is a great sameness in all the figures and hieroglyphics that are graven on the sacred buildings of Egypt. Here Rameses, introduced by some of the lesser deities into the presence of Ammon-Ra, presents his offerings ; and here Thoth, the god of letters, marks upon a palm-branch the victories obtained by the king. Ammon-Ra gives into his hand the symbol of life and power, and, presenting him with the sword and the sceptre, directs him, as the inscription informs us, to smite his foreign enemies with the one, and to rule Egypt with the other. Other sculptures show us a battle and a siege, and we see the king holding some captives by the hair of the head, whilst amongst the vanquished are groups of Asiatics, some of the conquered being evidently kings and queens, from their dress. On the walls of another chamber there is a procession of priests, bearing shrines. On the outer walls we have a battle scene. The king is in his chariot, and the reins are girded round his waist, his bow in his hand, and drawn ; and the arrow, winged with death, is about to leave the string, and to pierce the foe. On his right hand are two quivers, and the outer one is adorned with the figure of a lion. He drives his chariot wheels over captives, bowed and prostrate ; and his enemies fall before him and his soldiers like chaff before the wind. Here, on another part of the wall, you see the spoil which has been taken from the foe,—chariots and horses, oxen and asses ; and one of the latter beasts falls under the weight of a

bag of gold with which he is laden. On another
wall, Rameses pursues the enemy, who, in their flight
to the river, take refuge under the fortress of the
city ; some have already crossed the bridge over the
stream, and others are sinking in the blue waters.
One of the captains has been drowned, and his men
are trying to restore the lifeless corpse. They hold
his head downward, hoping by this means to expel
the water ; but their efforts are fruitless,—it is evident
that their chief is dead. The all-conquering Rameses
gains the victory, and his enemies, the Khitas, the
name given by the Egyptians to the Hittites, are
vanquished, and compelled to implore his mercy. On
the south wall of the great hall you see a battle, in
which a scaling ladder is used against a tower built
on a lofty rock, and where the besiegers are assailed
by the spears, and arrows, and stones of the be-
leaguered enemy ; but here again the Egyptians are
victorious, and the foe is put to the sword by the
king and his sons. Above these battle scenes are
processions of priests, who bear the figures of the
Theban ancestors of Rameses II. Here is also seen
the king cutting ears of corn, which is to be offered
to the god of life and organization ; and here is to be
seen the queen, and Apis, the sacred bull. On the
ceiling of another chamber, which is supposed to have

been the library of the palace, is an astronomical subject; and an inscription makes mention of the "Books of Thoth," the god of letters, and Saf, the lady of the sacred books. "This primitive Mercury is here attended," as Champollion records, "by a figure with an eye on his head, and surmounted by a legend, 'Sense of Light;' the goddess Saf being attended in like manner by a figure with an ear on his head, and labelled, 'Sense of Hearing.'" Champollion interprets these figures as indicators and guardians of the library—the Books of Thoth.[1]

There are many other sculptures on the walls of this temple, and here again, as in other temples, we see the king making offerings and burning incense to the gods; but those mentioned above are perhaps of the greatest interest, and are worthy of the closest inspection. As we trace the hand of the sculptor who finished his work thousands of years ago, we can only marvel at the greatness of his conception, and the delicacy of his ornament in so early an age of the world.

There is a tomb close to the Rameseum, and immediately behind it, which I visited several times.

---

[1] Miss Martineau: *Eastern Life, Present and Past*, chap. xiv. Edward Moxon, Dover Street. 1850.

It is known as the tomb of Rekhmara. It was
numbered by Sir G. Wilkinson as tomb 35, and the
number still remains. In the outer chamber there
is a long procession of Ethiopians and Asiatic chiefs,
bearing a tribute to Thothmes III. On a table are
offerings of the precious metals, rings and necklaces,
vessels of silver and vessels of gold, and other costly
ornaments, and the hieroglyphics tell us that they are
" chosen of the chief of the Gentiles of Kufa." But
not only do they bear with them rich and valuable
gifts, but they also bring with them monkeys, giraffes,
oxen with long horns, leopards, horses and dogs, and
ostrich feathers. Some of the chiefs are black, of the
negro type ; others of a red colour, like the Egyptians,
evidently from the south ; others who are clad in long
white garments are, as their features intimate, from
the north ; and some have their hair uncovered, and
others wear a cap which fits close on the head. Some
have long gloves with close sleeves, and are called
Rotennoo (the Assyrians), and behind these are their
wives, dressed in long robes, adorned with three sets
of flounces. It is very difficult, from the nature of the
lights—candles fixed upon long sticks, or now and
then a transient flash from the magnesium wire—to
make out the nature of the different figures on the
walls ; but we were able to see carpenters at work, K

and stone-masons who were putting the last touches
to a figure of the sphinx. Our attention was also
directed to the process of brick-making. The bricks
were placed in a mould, just as may be seen in Egypt
at the present day. Each brick was stamped with
the name of the king or high priest before it was
dried. Other pictures on the walls prove that there
is nothing new under the sun. Men who are heating
some liquid over a charcoal fire are using a pair of
bellows, though these are worked by the feet instead
of the hand. It is strange also to see on these walls
the glue, which has been heated on the fire, spread
with a brush upon pieces of wood which are to be
joined together. Here, too, may be noticed something of the domestic life of the ancient Egyptians;
for here is a maid-servant pouring out wine for a lady,
and returning an empty cup to a black slave. And
here may be seen some of their funeral customs, for
the mummy of a dead man is rowed by his servants
on a lake in a garden to his tomb, while a sacred
liturgy is being offered in his honour.

The tomb numbered 16 by Sir G. Wilkinson is
also full of interest. We have the names of four
kings, from Thothmes III. to Amenhotep III., which
is a point of importance, as settling the order of their
succession, and the order in which they appear is the
same as that given in the tablet of Abydos. We

have the judgment of "the Royal scribe" whose tomb
it is, before his admission to the presence of Osiris.
The funeral procession is seen advancing ; the coffin
containing the mummy of the dead is drawn on a
bier by four oxen ; the women are seen lamenting
over the deceased. Then follow men with various
offerings, and a priest, followed by the chief mourners,
performs the liturgy to the dead man, before the boats
in which are seated the Royal scribe and his sister.
On another wall are represented fowling and fishing
scenes ; in the outer chamber the Royal scribe, still
in the land of the living, is seated with his mother,
and he holds on his knee the infant daughter of
Amenhotep. Women dance to the sound of the
sistrum ; they offer flowers, they present costly perfumes ; and the servants bear in their hands goblets
of wine, which they give to the guests. The lower
part of the picture is devoted to the ceremonies of a
feast. One minstrel, seated cross-legged, plays on a
harp with seven strings ; another strikes a guitar, a
third is singing; while farther on an ox is being killed,
and the servants are preparing the different joints for
the banquet. It is evident that the hours fly with
winged feet ; there is music and mirth, singing and
dancing, laughter and pleasure, and all goes "merry
as a marriage bell." That the ancient Egyptians were
not only a grave and thoughtful people, as their

pictured scenes and literary remains assure us, but
that they were a light-hearted, pleasure-loving people
is evident from such sculptured incidents as those
described, and also from the account of them given
by Herodotus. He tells us that "they hold public
festivals, not only once in a year, but several times,"
and he gives us a description of a feast held in honour
of Diana in the city of Bubastis. "Now, when they
are being conveyed to the city Bubastis, they act as
follows : for men and women embark together, and
great numbers of both sexes in every barge ; some of
the women have castanets on which they play, and
the men play on the flute during the whole voyage,
the rest of the women and men sing and clap their
hands together at the same time. When in the course
of their passage they come to any town, they lay their
barge near to land, and do as follows : some of the
women do as I have described, others shout and scoff
at the women of the place ; some dance, and others
stand up and pull up their clothes ; this they do at
every town at the river-side. When they arrive at
Bubastis, they celebrate the feast, offering up great
sacrifices, and more wine is consumed at this festival
than in all the rest of the year. What with men and
women, beside children, they congregate, as the inhabitants say, to the number of 700,000."

THE VOCAL MEMNON (*Thebes*).

Memnon, thou'rt mute, thy voice is heard no more ;
    The rising sun now visits thee in vain.
    No music greets his coming ; ne'er again
Thy song shall float the Theban valley o'er,
Or thrilling reach the far Arabian shore,
    Never shall fill with music the wide plain.
    Methinks thy sightless eyes are full of pain,
Because thou art not as in days of yore.

Change hast thou seen, colossal Form in stone,
    Kings and their armies pass'd into the grave ;
Great dynasties destroyed, whose fame was blown
    Across whole continents, and o'er the wave,
    And nothing left the Founder's name to save,
But records traced on walls with weeds o'ergrown.

THE SILENT MEMNON.

A sweeter music, Memnon, far than thine
    Is heard since thou wast silent, for since then
    The Christ has lived, loved, died amongst us men,
So that the earth is now a sacred shrine,
Hallowed by that Great Presence all Divine,
    And from it hymns of praise rise up again,
    As once before in those far ages when
God's face in Paradise was seen to shine.

So if the old gods pass we do not mourn,
    Rather rejoice the false bears sway no more ;
That faiths have perished that were all out-worn,
    And in themselves seeds of corruption bore ;
That deities of all their glories shorn,
    Stand silent ever on Time's waveless shore.

CHAPTER XIV.

The Deir-el-Bahari Temple.—Sculptures on the Walls.—
Deir-el-Medineh.—Judgment Scene of Osiris.—Egyptians'
Belief in a Future Life.—Funeral Ceremonies.—" The Book
of the Dead."

A VERY impressive temple, one bearing no resemblance to any other, built near to some
great perpendicular rocks, and once approached
by a long avenue of sphinxes which no longer
exists, and by two obelisks of which only the base
remains, is Deir-el-Bahari, close to the Necropolis
of El-Assassif. Deir-el-Bahari, or Dayr-el-Bahri
as it is sometimes spelt, means "the Northern Convent"; for, like many of the temples at Thebes, it was
turned by the early Christians into a church and
monastery. It was raised in honour of Amen-noo-
het, better known as Queen Hatasou, the sister of
two kings of the 18th dynasty, Thothmes II. and
Thothmes III., with both of whom she for a short
time shared the throne. The sculptures on the walls
of her temple commemorate the expedition which she

sent into the land of Punt, or Arabia—a country celebrated for its gold and its ivory, its spices and its
scented gums. The principal episodes of that campaign are described in the bas-reliefs of Deir-el-Bahari.
The scene is laid on the sea-shore, and the fishes are
seen in the transparent water. Egyptian soldiers are
drawn up on the coast. The inhabitants of the Punt
country bring the produce of the soil; some pile
the scented gum in heaps; others bring entire trees,
the roots of which are tied up in baskets. The
Egyptian fleet is drawn up close by, and the ships,
propelled by sail and oar, are being loaded. Thebes
is at last reached, and we see the long procession of
monkeys, panthers, giraffes, and short-horned oxen;
while collars and chains, bracelets, daggers, and
hatchets are all being classed in order. Ammon
is witness of the scene, and addresses his congratulations to the Queen-Regent. In other chambers
other subjects are portrayed, and the scene lies on
the green waters of the Red Sea, and no longer on
the blue waters of the Nile.[1] Whether those episodes
belong to the same campaign, or to different ones, is
not certain, as there is nothing in the sculptures themselves to clear up this point. Mariette directs our

---

[1] Adapted from Mariette Bey's *Monuments of Upper Egypt.*

. attention to the freshness and vividness of the colours
in a chamber to which a fine doorway leads,—and on
each side of the passage to which, there is an admirable sculpture, representing a royal personage,   ˙
"who quenches his thirst with the milk of Hathor
under the form of the most beautiful cow that the
Egyptian bas-reliefs can show us."

Between the twin Colossi and Medinet-Habou, and
hidden in a hollow, is a small temple called Deir-el-
Medineh.   It was begun by Ptolemy Philopater,
and finished by his successor Physeon or Georgites
II.   The temple was dedicated by Philopater to
Hathor, the Egyptian Venus, " the President of the
West."   There are many sculptures and inscriptions
on the walls, and the usual offerings are being made
by the king to Ammon-Ra and Osiris. But that
which is worthy of most note in this temple, and
which marks it as a sepulchral monument, is the judgment scene of Osiris, which is so often described on
the papyrus rolls, which were placed with the mummy
in its coffin, and were called " Books of the Dead."
The spirit has entered the judgment-hall of Osiris,
who is seated on his throne, where he awaits the
arrival of the souls, which pass into Amenti, the
western region of the dead.   The dead man advances,
bearing in his hand the symbol of truth, an indication

of his meritorious deeds, and the assurances of his fitness to stand before Osiris. Thoth, the god of letters, carries in his hand a tablet, on which the actions of the deceased are noted down ; and one of the ministers of Thoth, in the form of an ape, and whose name is Hap (judgment), sits on the stand which supports the balance where the good deeds of the dead man are weighed against an ostrich feather.

These sculptures are full of the deepest interest, as teaching us something of the Egyptian's belief in a future life. There is not a doubt that they distinctly recognised the great facts of a life after death, the resurrection of the body, and a judgment to come. Indeed, a future world seems to have been much in their thoughts. The first thing which the king did when he began his reign was to begin his tomb. ' The inhabitants of this country," says Diodorus, " little value the short time of this present life, but put a high esteem upon the name and reputation of a virtuous life after death ; and they call the houses of the living *inns*, because they stay in them but a little while ; but the sepulchres of the dead they call *ever-lasting habitations*, because they abide in the grave to infinite generations. Therefore they are not very curious in the building of their houses, but in beautifying their sepulchres they leave nothing undone."

We know how it was customary at feasts for a
slave to carry round to all the guests the representation of a mummied corpse, and to show it to each in
turn, with the solemn words, " Look at this, and so eat
and drink ; for be sure that one day such as this thou
shalt be."¹ Some think that the practice of embalming the dead was an expression of the belief of the
ancient Egyptians in the immortality of the soul.
" The Ritual of the Dead," a copy of which was
placed with the mummy in his coffin, proves their
belief in a judgment to come. In one of the chapters
the spirit is seen hovering over the corpse, with a
human head, and human hands, in which it holds
the symbol of life and stability. According to Sir G.
Wilkinson, there was a lake near every city of importance for the transit of the dead, and a sacred boat
in waiting to bear the hearse across. The boatman,
whose official name was written in Greek, was Charon.
The funeral procession was compelled to cross the
lake, that the dead might pass through a human
ordeal of judgment before he was admitted to his
eternal habitation. Forty-two assessors on earth begin
the solemn work of judgment, which is to be con-
cluded by forty-two assessors in Amenti. The forty-
two earthly judges have notice given them of the
day of the funeral, and they await on the shores

of the lake over which the funeral procession is to pass, the arrival of the deceased and his friends. Any person may now come forward before these judges, and bring their accusations of immorality against the dead man ; and if the accusation be proved, his coffin is not permitted to be rowed across the lake ; while, if the accuser cannot make good his charge, he is punished with great severity. All were subject to the same ordeal, the highest as well as the lowest, the king as well as the priest. There was no exception, and all who were found guilty were refused admission into the sacred boat. The rejected were carried home, and their mummy-cases were placed upright against the wall of their chamber, where they remained a perpetual sorrow and shame to their families. If they chanced to be poor and friendless, they were buried on the borders of the lake, and here their melancholy ghosts wandered, longing in vain to enter the Elysian fields ; those fields being, according to Diodorus, " the beautiful meadows which in the principal burial-place of the Nile Valley at Memphis, extended beyond the Lake of the Dead, all flowery with lotus, and blossoming reeds."

Debtors were among those excluded from the rites of burial, and the creditor might seize the mummy till his claims were satisfied by the family, and the priest could even refuse a tomb till it was paid for. Herodotus tell us that so far back as the reign of "Asychis, who succeeded to the throne of Egypt after Mycerinus, son of Cheops, a king of the 4th dynasty, there was a law that a man could borrow money by giving in pledge the dead body of his father, and the lender was to have full power over the sepulture of the borrower ; and that if the debt was repudiated, he should not be buried in his family sepulture, or in any other, nor have the liberty of burying any others of his own dead." [1]

When the forty-two assessors permit the dead to be laid in the sacred boat, and to be ferried over the lake, an eulogy is pronounced on his character, and prayers are offered for his welfare in Hades by one of the officiating priests.   When the farther shore was reached, the ground was sprinkled before the wheels of the funeral car ; palm branches were strewn in the way, and the body was crowned with amaranth or fresh flowers.   Then the tomb was closed and sealed. The spirit, passing into Amenti, is met by Thoth, who leads him to a more terrible judgment than that by the shore of the lake where, by mortal judges, he has been declared fit for the habitations of blessed-

---

[1] Herodotus, ii. 136.

ness. Secret sins, sins of omission, sins of thought, on which man cannot pronounce judgment, now come under review; and Thoth produces the books in which he has recorded all the inner life of the man who is to be acquitted or condemned. Here are seen the forty-two judges, each representing one of the forty-two sins which, according to the belief of the Egyptians, man was subject to, and they examine the soul in respect to that particular sin. Then comes the trial of the balance. The heart is placed in one scale, the symbols of truth and justice in the other. The hawk-headed Thoth, the scribe of the gods, is present, ready to record the issue. Horus watches the scale in which the heart is placed, and at the same time eagerly scrutinizes the index of the balance. The dog-headed Anubis trims the opposite scale, and makes known the result of his scrutiny; and Thoth, who stands with his tablet and pen in front of Osiris, the supreme judge, records the sentence in his presence. Osiris, holding the sceptre and scourge, which symbolize justice and law, and seated in a shrine, wears a crown adorned with two ostrich feathers, and with the disc of the sun, and the horns of a goat. An altar, surmounted by the lotus flower, and laden with offerings probably presented by the relatives of the deceased, stands in front of the shrine.

On a pedestal not far from the throne, there is a hybrid creature, which has the body of a horse, the head of a crocodile, and the limbs of a lion ; and as he is called "the Devourer of Amenti," he is no doubt a minister of vengeance, ready to turn on the guilty man, if, when weighed in the balances, he shall be found wanting. If he pass the dread ordeal satisfactorily, Osiris welcomes him by raising the end of his sceptre, and he is permitted to enter the realms of joy. There the righteous dwell in everlasting bliss, reaping the corn in the meadows of Paradise, gathering the fruits from its trees, and bathing in the pure river of life that waters the mansions of glory. If he cannot endure the ordeal, then he is sent back to earth in the form of a wolf, or scorpion, or, lowest state of all, of a pig, to pass thousands of years— three or ten—in this horrible condition of transmigration, before he is released, and permitted to return to his human body once more. We see, then, from " The Book of the Dead," that the old Egyptians had a very distinct idea of a future life. Copies of the book are to be seen in the British Museum. This book, which was in use many thousand years ago, was intended as a sort of guide to the dead in the mummy stage of existence, giving instructions as to their passage into that "undiscovered country from whose bourne no traveller returns." Here, too, we find the hymns that were sung, and the prayers that were offered, as the mummy was lowered into the grave, with directions as to the amulets to be placed with it in its case, and the cloths in which it was to be wrapped. "The mummy-cloths, to which great mystical importance was attached, were made of the finest linen, and were sometimes beautifully embroidered in needlework of various colours ; and it is said that some of them have been unrolled to the length of 1,000 yards, and that there is no form of bandage known to modern surgery of which instances may not be found on the mummies."[1]

---

[1] Zincké's *Egypt.*

CHAPTER XV.

IT has been often asked, Whence did the Egyptians derive their conceptions of a future life? Was it from some lingering tradition of a primeval revelation? Or was it because the belief of a future life is a natural instinct in the heart of man, to which he is guided by the light, both of reason and of conscience? The faith is common to men of all countries and climes, that the soul, immortal in its longings, survives the stroke of death; and the Egyptians, more than other nations who had no revelation, had clear ideas on the subject. Some would have us believe that they had even clearer conceptions of a future life than the Hebrews, and that the Mosaic Scriptures ignore a future state of rewards and punishments. This I am unable to accept, for though it was Christ who "brought life

and immortality to light by the Gospel," yet I cannot read the Old Testament without seeing that the
hope of immortality burned brightly amid the shadows of the earlier dispensation. I firmly believe that
"the old Fathers did not look only for transitory
promises," and that their hope was not bounded by
the horizon of time. Once and again in the sacred
writings is the eternal inheritance spoken of as the
object of their desire. The author of the Epistle to
the Hebrews tells us that Abraham " looked for a city
which hath foundations, whose builder and maker is
God." He says of all those who, like " the father of
the faithful," confessed that they were strangers and
pilgrims on the earth, that "they desired a better
country, that is, an heavenly : wherefore God is not
ashamed to be called their God : for He hath prepared
for them a city." The translation of Enoch, and the
rapture of Elijah, must have given a clear testimony
to the men of their day that there is a life to come—a
state in which the corruptible shall put on incorrup-
tion, and the mortal be clothed with immortality.
Indeed, Christ Himself assures us that not only life
after death, but the resurrection of the body, was
revealed indirectly, at least in the early days, and
revealed through the covenant relationship which God
held towards the Hebrew nation. He states in L

evidence of this the fact that God calls Himself "the God of Abraham, and of Isaac, and of Jacob." The Sadducees denied the resurrection of the dead. "Now that the dead are raised, even Moses showed at the first, when he calleth the Lord, the God of Abraham, and the God of Isaac, and the God of Jacob. For He is not the God of the dead, but of the living: for all live unto Him." His reasoning is this. All the holy men of old who died in the faith are living still, awaiting in the presence of God the resurrection; for as the covenant promises were made to them while they . were in the flesh, so must they rise in the flesh to receive their fulfilment. The grave cannot hold them for ever, for they must, as God is true to His word, come forth and enjoy the city which He has prepared for their everlasting habitation. It is true that David sometimes speaks of death as the end, and asks, "Wilt Thou show wonders to the dead? Shall the dead arise and praise Thee?" But this is only when he cries from "the depths," and he is troubled by the mysteries and problems of life; for at other times he stands on the Pisgah height of hope, and as the land of promise stretches out before him, he exclaims in the clear tones of joy: "My heart is glad, and my glory rejoiceth: my flesh also shall rest in hope. For Thou wilt not leave my soul in hell; neither wilt Thou

suffer Thine Holy One to see corruption. Thou wilt
show me the path of life : in Thy presence is fulness
of joy; at Thy right hand there are pleasures for
evermore."

Solomon, who shows us "the vanity" of things here,
and "the vexation of spirit" which accompanies even
the most coveted things of this earth, cannot be said,
as I have seen it stated by Zincké in his suggestive
book on Egypt, to pass over the future life, "as not
thinking it worth even a passing reference." If in
times of mental gloom and despondency, natural to a
man who had lived so much for this present world, its
pomps, and pleasures, and enjoyments, he says, "For
to him that is joined to all the living there is a hope ;
for a living dog is better than a dead lion ; for the
living know that they shall die, but the dead know not
anything, neither have they any more a reward, for
the memory of them is forgotten," at another time
he speaks clearly of a future state for man, and of
judgment to come ; for he winds up the sad book of
Ecclesiastes, full as it is of doubts and questionings,
with this distinct statement, which surely has a bearing on the sanctions of another life: ' For God shall
bring every work into judgment, with every secret
thing, whether it be good, or whether it be evil"
(Eccles. xii. 14).

I suggest as a reason why future rewards and punishments were not attached to the Mosaic code, that, had they been so, the Israelites would have been led to think that salvation came by the law. If heaven had been promised as the recompense of obedience to the commandments, then the natural conclusion would have been that the sinner i s saved, not by grace, but by works. But however this may be, and believing that " Christ brought life and immortality to light through His gospel," shedding illumination on man's true and endless life, and making it stand out more distinctly as an object of faith and hope than ever it had done i n the early dispensation ; yet I cannot believe that the Hebrew Scriptures either ignore or reject the hopes and fears connected with the world to come. With the full assumption that God was the Legislator, and often the Executor of His own law i n the Mosaic dispensation, and that He often punished violations of the law visibly and at once ; yet there is nothing in this to militate against the truth that, " both in the Old and New Testaments, everlasting life is offered to mankind by Christ, and that the old Fathers did not look for transitory promises only."

I think I need hardly say that the teaching of the prophets, though this is denied by some, is pervaded by this paramountly influential and morally vital idea

of a future life. It appears to me that they everywhere build on this all-important truth, and that it
runs through their writings like a thread of gold,
though brighter and more conspicuous at one time
than another. But this does not lessen the wonder of
the truth that these old Egyptians, by some means or
other, grasped the grand idea of a future life, when
the soul that had been tried in the balance, and not
found wanting, passed into the eternal light, and
when the soul that had succumbed to temptation, and
been defiled by pollution, was given over to the forty-
two avenging demons, types of the vices and crimes
the sinner had indulged and committed, and which
should be his tormentors for ever.

CHAPTER XVI.

THE most southern of the temples of Thebes is the vast pile of Medinet-Habou.   It was built by Rameses III.   This king says to one of his gods, as recorded in the great Harris Papyrus, " I built for thee thy divine abode in the midst of its area, fabricating and making the construction of square stone ; its doors and its lintels were of gold, nailed together with brass.   I inlaid it with precious stones, like the belt of heaven."

The tomb of this monarch in the Valley of the Kings is known as " Bruce's tomb," and has been already described.   It is one of the most impressive of the Egyptian temples.   According to Mariette, Medinet-Habou is composed of two separate temples —the first, the temple of Thothmes III., belonging to the Roman period, " as the florid capitals of the

columns standing at the end of the first court, and also
the clumsy style of the sculptures, and especially of
the hieroglyphs, clearly indicate." [1]   The names of
Titus, Hadrian, and Antoninus may be read in various
parts of the court.

You enter the temple of Rameses III. through two
immense pylons leading to two spacious courts, both
open to the sky.   The first court has a covered colonnade at each side, and on the right is a row of seven
pillars, bearing the figure of Osiris, or rather Rameses
III. in the attributes of Osiris ; and to the left are
eight similar columns, with capitals representing the
graceful papyrus plant.   The same court is surrounded
by a peristyle, supported on the east and west by
five massive columns, while to the south is a row of
eight Osiride pillars ; and on the north side is a
similar number.   This court was once used as a Christian church, and the centre is still encumbered by
some Roman pillars, which contrast unfavourably
with the grandeur of the Osiride pillars and the gigantic columns.   A plan of this temple, with the measurements of its various courts, and a minute description
of its sculptures, and the scenes pictured on its walls,
is given in Murray's *Handbook of Egypt.*   Miss

---

[1] Mariette's *Monuments of Upper Egypt*, p. 202.

Edwards, in her *Thousand Miles up the Nile*, gives some very interesting details of these wonderful ruins. I will therefore only draw the attention of the reader to a few of the scenes depicted in the various chambers which I consider the most striking, and which every visitor to Medinet-Habou should make a point of examining with care.

On the wall of the building known as the Pavilion, you see the home life of Rameses III. He is seated ; his attendants stand before him. One lady offers him flowers ; another waves a fan ; a third, who has just presented him with some fruit, he caresses ; and with another he is playing chess or draughts, and the hand of the lady is on the piece she is about to move.

Then on some of the walls are battle scenes, in which Rameses is always victorious, and where he is represented as bringing to the gods the prisoners he has captured in war. The captives are of various nations. Some are from Libya and Palestine ; some are natives of Sardinia, and others of Tuscany. The representative of the Libyans, described as "the vile chief of the Khetas," is full-faced and beardless ; his ears are adorned with large rings, and his head is covered with a tight-fitting cap, from which falls a tress of hair which hangs down his back. "The vile chief of the Amaro country has a long face and pointed beard. This is the king of the Amorites, the inhabitants of the western shores of the Dead Sea."[1] Passing by the portraits of other captives, which, as Mariette says, "must have been drawn from the life," I come to "the chief of the vile race of Kousch. The artist has exceptionally given him the features of a negro, although Kousch was more accurately included by the Egyptians themselves in the Chamitic race." Many of the European nations are depicted elsewhere on the walls, and among the captives led by Rameses III. into the presence of Ammon-Ra are Pelasgi and men of other Western tribes, with features of a refined and classical type, and wearing the national costume. The knowledge that we gain from these sculptures is really great and important. "With much remarkable skill," says Mariette, "the Egyptian sculptor has succeeded in giving to each one of these prisoners the distinctive type of his race. We must remember that we are here in the 13th century before our era, and the ethnologist will nowhere find more authentic specimens of the nations who then inhabited Western Asia, Libya, and the Soudan."

Not only are wars on land represented on the walls of this temple, but we have the picture of a sea-fight,

---

[1] Mariette's *Monuments of Upper Egypt*, p. 206.

in which the Egyptian galleys win the victory over the maritime nations of the Mediterranean.

On another wall there is a coronation scene, which is thus described by Champollion: "Rameses quits his palace, carried in a richly decorated shrine borne by twelve military chiefs, whose heads are adorned with ostrich feathers. Decorated with all the marks of his sovereign power, he is seated on a throne, which golden images of truth and justice overshadow with their wings. Standing near the throne, which they seem to protect, are the sphinx, emblem of wisdom combined with strength, and the lion, emblem of courage. Officers wave around the shrine flabella and fans; young children of the sacerdotal caste march near the king, carrying his sceptre, the case for his bow, and other insignia. There follow him princes of the royal blood, priests, and warriors who carry the pedestals, and the steps of the shrine. The king is preceded by a band of music and chorus singers, followed by his friends and relations, among whom are several high priests; and his eldest son, second in command of the army, burns incense before his father's face. When the king arrives at the temple of Horus, he approaches the altar, pours out the libations and burns incense; and twenty-two priests carry upon a rich palanquin the statue of the god, which is borne forward surrounded by flabella and fans and flowering branches. The king, on foot, crowned with the simple diadem of the Lower country, precedes the god, and follows closely the white bull, the living symbol of Ammon-Horus and Ammon-Ra, his mother's consort. A priest waves incense before the sacred animal. The queen, from an elevated position, witnesses all this religious pomp. Then comes the scene of the four birds, which are genii, children of Osiris, and patrons of the four cardinal priests. The high priest lets them fly, in order that they may proclaim to the south and to the north, to the west and to the east, that, following the example of the god Horus, Rameses has crowned himself with the emblems of his dominion over the Upper and Lower countries. The last part of the bas-relief represents the king, crowned with the pschent, or crown of Upper and Lower Egypt, giving thanks to the god in his temple. The monarch, preceded by the entire sacerdotal body, and military chiefs, and attended by the officers of his household, cuts some ears of corn with a golden sickle, and pouring out a libation, takes leave of the god Ammon-Horus, who has retired within his sanctuary. The queen again looks on at these ceremonies ; the priest invokes the gods ; a priestly scribe reads a prayer ; and the white bull, and the images of the king's royal ancestors, are seen once more side by side with the Pharaoh." [1]

This large temple of Rameses III., or Medinet-Habou, may challenge comparison with any other of the Egyptian monuments for interest, whether we consider its immense pylons and magnificent courts, the sculptures and hieroglyphics on its various chambers, or the beauty and freshness of the colours on its pictured walls.

After a close study of the temple, I climbed the mound on the western side, where considerable excavations have been carried on, and near which are the remains of an old Coptic village. You get a view from it of the surrounding country, the desert sands, the cultivated fields, the waters of the Nile, and in the distance, towards the south, the remains of an old Coptic church. There is an expanse of depressed soil near the temple, with alluvial deposits round its edges, which Sir G. Wilkinson thinks may have been the Lake of the Dead, across which the mummy was ferried in the sacred boat.

It is in the second court of Medinet-Habou that, after inspecting the doorways and the pylons, and the various groups of pictures, and ascending the crum-

---

[1] Curtailed from Champollion's *Lettres Ecrites d'Egypte.*

bling mounds, we find our dragoman has provided luncheon, and we are glad of rest and refreshment under the shadow of the pillared colonnade. The sky on a midwinter day was cloudless, and the sun shone down from burning skies. The glare of the hot sand made the eyes ache ; and the shade was most grateful, as was also a draught of the cool Nile water which the little Arab girl, my smiling attendant, bore in a goollch on her head.

CHAPTER XVII.

AFTER resting awhile, and casting another look upon the grand pillars and colonnades, we again mounted our donkeys, and riding past plots of wheat and barley, and through the sweet bean-fields now in blossom, we turned our faces eastward, and saw the two Colossi which once guarded the temple of Amenophis III., a king of the 18th dynasty, rising up side by side amidst the green plain. Eighteen similar statues, forming a grand and majestic avenue of approach to the palace of the king, and whose fragments lie in the fields behind, turned their still and solemn faces towards the sunrise. Each of these statues, as also the two Colossi, represented Amenophis himself. Of the temple before which they stood as sentinels, there is not a trace. The Colossi were originally monoliths. We learn from Strabo that, in the year 27 B.C., the upper part of the Colossus known as the Memnon, and which is on the northern side of the other, was destroyed by an earthquake. It is now built from the waist upwards, with a mass of stones moulded into the shape of a human head and body. Some think that Cambyses, the Persian king, in his hatred of idols, and an excess of religious zeal, destroyed this Colossus, as they imagine he shattered the colossal figure of Rameses in the Rameseum. The faces of both are dreadfully mutilated and marred. Whatever was the cause of the ruin wrought upon the Memnon,—and it may be asked, would not an earthquake have buried both the statues with their pedestals beneath the sand ?—the damage it received proved the cause of the Memnon's fame. For when the rays of the morning sun touched the headless statue, there was heard a sweet sound, as that of a human voice. This is said to have been the effect of heat on the splintered and cold stone, wet with the morning dew. Others say that a crafty priest hid himself in a recess which still exists in the body of the statue, and that he there struck a metallic-sounding stone. In order to test the probability of this, I got an Arab to climb the statue, place himself in its lap, and strike the stone with his staff. There

was a very distinct ring, both metallic and clear, I
thought. However, the Greeks and Romans who
then visited the Nile regarded the musical sound as
miraculous. They ascribed the morning song to the
son of Tithonus, who, with plaintive voice, was invoking his divine mother, Aurora.

The fame of the vocal Memnon soon spread abroad,
and people came from all parts of the known world ;•
among them, as the inscriptions on the statue inform
us, " Sabina Augusta, the consort of the Emperor
Cæsar Augustus (Hadrian), who testifies that she
has twice heard the voice of Memnon during the
first hour." The Emperor Hadrian himself paid his
homage to the statue, which, rejoicing at his presence, "uttered a sound a third time." The earliest
of the inscriptions dates from the reign of Nero, and
the most recent from the reign of Septimus Severus.
This emperor, in order to stop the plaintive cries of
the Memnon, and to give clearness to his voice, re-
paired the statue, but, alas! silenced it under the
layers of sandstone piled together for its restoration.

These impressive statues, 64 feet 4 inches high,
with their pedestals—the figures at the side representing the mother and wife of Amenophis—sit
solitary, with their hands on their knees, amidst an
expanse of verdure. At the annual inundation of

the Nile they look from their pedestals unmoved and untroubled, and their gigantic shadows fall on a waste of waters. In the old times of the splendour of Thebes, the Nile did not rise so high, and the water of the sacred river did not wash even their feet, and they sat among the sphinxes, and pylons, and pillars of the temple of Amenophis, on a raised platform, gazing across the sands and the plain. But the bed of the Nile has risen since those days, and in proportion to its elevation the waters have spread over the level desert and fields, and the pedestals of the great Colossi have been buried deeper and deeper in the alluvial deposit of the river. I never visited the Theban plain without riding round by "the Pair," and spending some time in looking at those sublime figures which have stood there for thousands of years, unchanging amid change, unmoved by the rise and fall of dynasties, unaffected by the revolutions which, since they were placed on their thrones by a mighty king, have turned the world upside-down. There have they sat, keeping watch and ward over the plain; and there they may sit, tranquil and undisturbed, till the sands shall run out from the hour-glass of time. On my last visit it was a brilliant afternoon, and the heat was tempered by some fleecy clouds that floated across the sky. The

M

Arabian hills were glowing in the distance, the lights of a faint rose, the shadows of a deep purple ; while in the foreground lay the yellow sands, and the deep green plain, and feathery palms, and the blue waters of the Nile flowing tranquilly along. It was a scene of great beauty ; and over it, from their lofty thrones, kept watch the solitary pair.

THE TWIN COLOSSI.

These two through ages have been sitting here,
Two solemn forms of one great king in stone,
The plinth beneath them serving for a throne.
Here they have reigned as passed each passing year,
Unmoved by hope, untroubled by a fear.
With eyes that fain would pierce to lands unknown,
Beyond the burning sand-dunes waste and drear,
Watchers they are across the desert lone.

Seated with hands upon their knees imprest,
Did they not symbolise to all who came,
Eternal silence and eternal rest ?
For though the world might change, they sat the same
In grandeur immemorial ever drest,
And robed in majesty beyond all name.

CHAPTER XVIII.

LEAVING what I have to say about a prolonged
stay at Luxor till my return from the Second
Cataract, I should like to take the reader—may I
say the gentle reader?—with me on my delightful
passage up the Nile.

The hills, which had withdrawn from the river
both on the eastern and western sides, forming a
circle round the wide green plain, which here
stretches on each side the Nile to an unusual extent,
begin now to close in again, and the valley gradually
becomes once more only a narrow strip of cultivated
land. Indeed, this is the character of the scenery all
along the upper valley of the Nile. A brown moun-

tain background, a scanty patch of vegetation, a bank
sloping greenly down to the water's edge, and in the
background a group of palms. The Dôm palm,
which is not found south of the Thebaid, is now
frequently seen, and, as a tree, is not so beautiful as
its congener, the date palm. The latter tree is not
only a picturesque object in the landscape, but every
part of it can be made serviceable. Its leaves are
used for mats and baskets, the fibre for ropes, the
trunk for beams, and the fruit for food. The Dôm
palm is an eccentric-looking tree. The trunk divides
at some four or five feet from the ground; each
branch separates into two others, and these again
bifurcate; and so the pairs are multiplied till the
extreme ends are terminated in radiating groups of
fan-like leaves. It bears hard, brown-coloured nuts,
which hang in clusters, and the kernel is used as
vegetable ivory, and from it buttons and ornaments
are made. On account of the meagre vegetation of
the Nile some miles above Thebes, the population
is scanty; few villages meet the eye, and the banks
are lonely and silent, save where at times a shadoof
is at work, and its harsh and melancholy sound falls
on the ear. For some time, however, after we leave
Luxor, the valley is fertile and well-peopled. There
are green fields and prosperous towns, and we pass

Erment, with its sugar factories and gardens, which
I visited on my return from Wady Halfa to Luxor,
and Mutanch, where we come upon a beautiful bend
of the Nile, and some detached hills known as the
Gebelyn. We reached Esneh, which is thirty-seven
miles from Luxor, in about four hours and a half,
and went on shore to visit the temple, which is in
the middle of the town. Esneh is the capital of the
province, the abode of a pasha, and a town of some
importance. The chief employment of the people
is dyeing blue cotton ; and as you pass through the
market-place to the temple, you see large pieces of
this material hanging out to dry on ropes which are
stretched overhead. All that is now to be seen of the
temple is a large portico, supported by columns, which
belongs to the Roman period, leading to a hypostyle
hall, which has been cleared out to the very basis
of the pillars. A large portion of the temple lies
buried under the houses of the town. The portico
bears the cartouches of several of the Roman emperors, beginning with Claudius. But what is most
worthy of note are the richly carved capitals of the
columns, where the palm-leaf takes the place of the
lotus, and the ceiling in which the zodiac is painted ;
for the sculptures of the Ptolemaic times are poor in
execution, and show how rapidly the engraver's art

had begun to decline. The gods seem no longer objects of awe and reverence as in the olden days, for they condescend to conduct the kings to the sports of the field, catching birds or fish, or driving before them bulls and goats, and flocks of geese.

Esneh did not detain us long, and returning to the boat we pursued our passage as far as Edfou, a distance of thirty-two miles from Esneh, and 532 from Cairo. Here the steamer anchored for the night. Long before we had reached the landing-place we had seen the lofty pylon of the temple, towering 120 feet high from the green fields that lie around the modern village. We landed and found donkeys in readiness for those who wished to ride the short distance which separates the river from the most perfectly preserved temple in Egypt, some preferring to walk through the fields, and over the plank that crosses the great canal. As you pursue your way, you come to a part of the road where, winding by the narrow mud houses of the village, you lose sight of the magnificent pylon, and then advancing a few yards the temple bursts into view. The temple is now set free from the houses of the village, which had invaded it on every side, choking it up with rubbish, and it can be seen in all its architectural details, while the inscriptions are laid bare to the

scrutiny of the antiquarian. It is the only temple in
Egypt which stands in its original perfection, complete as the architects left it. The temple was founded
by Ptolemy Philopater, and dedicated to " Horus
of the Winged Disc." Ptolemy built the various
courts, the sanctuary, and the chapel; his successors
added the decorations of the inner chambers, and
an inscription records that the temple, begun under
Philopater, finished under Euergetes II., was completed, after interruptions caused by wars, in ninety-
five years. Mariette thinks "that this statement can
apply to the actual construction only, and not to the
decorations, since from the beginning of the reign of
Philopater to the death of Dionysos, the last of the
kings whose cartouches appear in the temple, no less
than 170 years elapsed. There is a close resemblance
in its construction and details' between this temple
and the temple of Denderah ; both are beautiful, and
richly decorated, though Edfou is the more perfect
of the two. It is a pleasant circumstance that we
know who was the architect of so noble a building,
for he has put his name to his work ; " and that name
was Ei-em-hotep-Oer-si-Phtah (Imouthes, the great
son of Phtah).[1] You look with interest on the

---

[1] Mariette Bey : *The Monuments of Upper Egypt.*

sanctuary, with its massive granite shrine, formed of
a single block, in which the sacred hawk, symbol of
Horus, the military god, was jealously concealed.
After some time spent in examining the hypostyle
hall, and the decorations of the chambers, we climbed
to the top of the twin towers by a winding staircase
of 240 steps. The ascent to the roof is easy, but
were it difficult, the labour would be amply rewarded.
You look down into the great courts surrounded by
sculptured columns, with their graceful capitals, and
beyond is the noble hypostyle hall, while round the
corridor run lofty and sculptured walls which spring
from the pylon. Looking away from the temple, and
over the mud village at your feet, with its flat
roofs, and little yards where half-naked children
are at play, you see a wide expanse of country,
a stretch of yellow sand running up to the green
fields, and the Nile flowing like a thread of silver,
and gleaming in the noonday sun. After you have
satisfied " the lust of the eye," you descend again
by the winding staircase, and, loath to leave the
beautiful temple, you examine the sculptures again ;
for to these Miss Edwards, in her delightful book, has
especially directed your attention. These sculptures
have merely to do with the ceremonies of religion,
and the offerings of kings to the gods, though in one

corridor you see the harpooning of the hippopotamus, and in several instances the harpooner has struck his weapon into one of the attendants instead of the animal which it was intended to wound.   But they have an especial value of their own.   " There are here more inscriptions of a miscellaneous character than in any temple of Egypt, and it is precisely this secular information that is to us so priceless.   Here are geographical lists of Nubian and Egyptian nomes, with their principal cities, their products, and their tute- lary gods ; lists of tributary provinces and princes ; lists of temples, and of the lands pertaining thereunto ; lists of canals, of ports, of lakes ; kalendars of feasts and fasts ; astronomical tables, genealogies and chron- ologies of the gods ; lists of the priests and the priestesses of both Edfou and Denderah, with their names ; lists also of singers and assistant function- aries; lists of offerings, hymns, invocations ; and such a profusion of religious legends as make of the walls of Edfou alone a complete text-book of Egyptian mythology." [1]

We left Edfou early in the morning, and in a few hours reached Gebel-el-Silsileh, where the Nile is shut in by two mountains, and where are the quarries from

[1] *One Thousand Miles up the Nile.*

which was cut the stone for the temples and palaces of Thebes.   Ranges of red sandstone now succeed to limestone cliffs.   Gebel-el-Silsileh means "the hill of the chain," for it is said that a king once barred the river here with a chain.   The quarries on the right bank are the most extensive, and it is very interesting to observe the extreme care and the nice method with which the rock has been quarried, the stone being cut with the same regularity as a carpenter would use in planing the trunk of a tree.   In some places the marks made by the masons' tools 3,000 years ago are plainly visible,—these remain, though the hand that cut the huge blocks has long been turned into dust.   On the left bank the rocks are honeycombed with grottos, and there is a large speos with four massive pillars, dating from the reign of Horus, a king of the 18th dynasty.   As the Nile was here the object of a special worship, because as some think the river narrows between the banks, and runs with a strong current, solemn hymns addressed to the river are engraved on the rocks.   There are some sculptures of great interest, and here we see a bas-relief of a goddess nourishing the infant King Horus with her divine milk, and on another wall is pictured the triumph of Horus, who has conquered the Ethiopians, or Cushites, riding in his royal chariot, beside which strolls a lordly lion. Armed soldiers attend him, prisoners follow, and the king holds some of the vanquished foe by the hair.

We take to the boat again, and as we look around us from the deck, we see that the valley has shrunk to a narrow strip of green. In a short time we reach Kom Ombo, about fifteen miles from Gebel-el-Sil-sileh. It stands solitary on the edge of a cliff on the eastern bank overlooking the river and the valley. Kom Ombo, which crowns the precipitous bank, was rebuilt by the Ptolemies on the site of an ancient temple of the date of the Pharaohs of an early part of the Third Period, and bears the name of Philo-meter, of Euergetes II., and of Dionysos. It consists indeed of two temples, and, strange to say, though placed side by side, they are dedicated to gods as eternally antagonistic as are the principles of good and evil : the one has Horus, the god of light, for its tutelary deity ; the other is dedicated to Sebek, the crocodile god, who symbolizes darkness. It is thought that this temple will soon disappear, and that the sand-drifts from the desert will ere long bury the whole, as they have already submerged the bases of the columns. All who have visited this impressive shrine must regret that such a doom awaits it.

A pleasant passage of twenty-seven miles, through

scenery novel in its character, black syenite rocks jutting out from the river on all sides, and we reach the most southern town in Egypt—Assouan. This is the old Syene, and just below it the Nile is divided into two streams by the island of Elephantine. In early Egyptian inscriptions Assouan was called Abu, "town of the elephant;" hence the name of the island, Elephantine. Lunnu, the name of the town in the time of the Ptolemies, must have been, as Dr. Wallis Budge says, "the recognised name of the place as early as the time of Ezekiel, for this prophet defines the northern and southern limits of Egypt by the words 'from Migdol to Syene' (Ezek. xxix. 10, *margin*). The words 'from Migdol to Syene' meant all Egypt, just as 'from Dan to Beersheba' meant all Palestine." "Apart from the importance of Assouan," says the same authority, "as a military station and frontier town, it obtained great notoriety among the ancients, from the fact that Eratosthenes and Ptolemy considered it to be in the Tropic of Cancer, and the most northerly point where, at the time of the summer solstice, the sun's rays fell vertically, so that objects such as trees and animals cast no shadow there ; also the day was said to be 13½ hours long in this place.

"In the times of the Ptolemies there was a famous

well there, into which the sun was said to shine at the summer solstice, sending his rays perpendicularly into it, and illuminating it in every part, and the sun was said to fit the well like the cover of a vessel."

Assouan is the frontier town of Egypt proper. Here another country begins. It was interesting to go on shore, and to find one's self among a crowd of Nubians and Egyptians, negroes and Bedouins. The Nubians are a fine-looking race, black as night, but well formed, and with intelligent faces. The shore was lined with people selling their wares—elephants' tusks, and ostrich feathers, ornaments of silver and glass, pikes and lances, and arrows, the points of which are said to be poisoned, and whips made of hippopotamus hide. There were camels and donkeys on the bank all ready saddled, and only waiting for riders ; and very soon I saw gentlemen and ladies mounted on " the ship of the desert," looking anxious and uncomfortable, and, if one might judge from their appearance, feeling insecure. They did not trust themselves wholly to the snarling beasts, but had a man or boy to lead the animal. Instead of trading on the shore, I walked under the shadow of some fine acacia trees, and past some coffee-shops, and through a narrow lane, under the escort of a half-naked black boy, to the only bazaar in the town.

Here there is a large assortment of elephants' tusks
and leopard skins, of strong sticks and ebony clubs,
of strings of beads and silver bracelets, of ostrich
feathers, and black girdles made of leather and
adorned with white shells, and well saturated with
castor oil. These girdles form the only dress of a
Nubian girl. The scanty garment is known as a
"Madam Nubia." But the articles just mentioned do
not form the only merchandise in the bazaar, for if
you are so disposed you may buy the red and black
baskets of the country, and slippers of all colours,
and shawls and handkerchiefs which have a strangely
familiar appearance, and which, with cotton goods,
are much prized in Assouan, for they come all the
way from Manchester. The castor-oil plant grows
here, and the oil is much used by the Nubian belles,
who soak their hair i n it after it has been plaited
into innumerable and elaborate curls. They are
evidently proud of their black and corkscrew tresses.

Opposite to Assouan, and on the western side of
the river, is the island of Elephantine. Here the
small population i s entirely Nubian. The island is
eminently disappointing ; for as you know that it is
called by the natives " Geyeeretez Zaher," " the island
of flowers," and as you have heard marvellous tales of
its beauty, you expect a little Eden of loveliness and

verdure ; whereas you find brown, sun-baked mounds, the ruins of an old town, and a modern village built of mud. Bits of broken pottery, many of them bearing Greek inscriptions, are scattered about ; and were it not for some groups of palms and a few patches of verdure, the island would present the appearance of unrelieved ugliness. There are the ruins of a granite gateway, bearing the name of Alexander III., a coarsely cut statue of Osiris, with the cartouche of Menephtah, and the remains of a Nilometer, which shared the fate of two temples, and was partly destroyed by one of the governors of Assouan, who removed some of the stones in order to build a palace. From the south side of Elephantine we catch our first sight of the First Cataract. The cataract is really no cataract in the customary sense of the word, and he who hopes to see a second Niagara with its grand " sweep of seething billowy sea," or a Vellino with its " hell of waters " rapid as the light, will be grievously disappointed. This is a rapid rather than a cataract. The river is full of little rocks and islets, round which the water foams and eddies, making a succession of small whirlpools ; and the current, as it hurries down the gradual descent of the stream, is both swift and strong. You see but a small part of the cataract, however, from Elephantine—only a section of its weird and desolate surroundings. One must go up to Mahattah, just above the rapids, and see the torrent from thence, and shoot it in a small boat, before it is possible to understand the wildness of the scene, or the excitement that attends the descent in a canoe. We shot the cataract on our return from Wady Halfa, and I leave further remarks on the tumult of the waters until I have had the pleasure of being carried safely down the whirling and rushing stream.

"WHERE ARE THE GREAT AND SCEPTRED KINGS?"

Where are the great and sceptred kings of yore,
  Who carried wars and conquests far and wide,
  And built their temples near that dusky tide
Which plants a green oasis on the shore ?
Oh, where the suppliants who off'rings bore
  To Pasht and Isis, gods to whom they cried,
  Or to the sacred bulls they deified ?
Gone are their pomp and pride for evermore.

Where are the maidens once as Hathor fair,
  With whom these conquerors had loved to toy,
Girls sweet as lotus-blossom in their hair,
  Who filled the world with laughter and with joy ?
  Withered the beauty men thought could not cloy,—
The charms that stung their rivals to despair.

CHAPTER XIX.

A S we were about to go as far as the Second
Cataract, we left our large, comfortable boat,
the *Rameses*, at Assouan, and proceeded to Philæ,
where we were to go on board a smaller steamship,
the *Seti*, to make our passage through Nubia to Wady
Halfa, the extreme frontier of Egypt to the south,
and beyond which travellers cannot proceed farther
up the Nile.

There are three ways of reaching Philæ from
Assouan ; you may ascend the cataract, or ride across
the desert, or take the railway. We chose the second
way, in order to see the famous quarries from which
was hewn the granite for the obelisks, the colossal
statues of Rameses, the tombs of the sacred bulls,
and the temples and palaces of Thebes, as well as
for the coating of the Third Pyramid, and the temple
of the Sphinx. It is an impressive ride. On leaving

N

the town the Arab cemetery, with gravestones inscribed in Kufic characters, is passed, looking arid and
baked, neglected and dreary, as all Mohammedan
burial places are ; and some ruined mosques are seen
here and there, with their arching domes.   In this
cemetery the first Muezzin of Islam is said to be buried.
You pass, too, a little English cemetery, well kept
and tended, and green with verdure, for the ground
close by is irrigated, and rice and corn are growing
near ; and here some English soldiers lie, who died
from fever, the climate being intensely hot in the
summer.   Then you ride through a dreary desert of
sand, on each side of which crop up great gloomy
masses of granite, and purple syenite, many of which
assume the most grotesque shapes and the weirdest
forms.   We now reach the quarries, out of which every
monument in Egypt was hewn, and was then floated
down the river from the place from which it was
taken—with what amount of labour and skill who can
tell ?—to the site where it was to stand.   There is
one obelisk in the quarry now, hewn out, but never
removed from its granite bed—why, no one can say.
The name of the king who wished it to be separated
from its native block, and raised to his honour, is
unknown.   Had it been finished, this huge monolith,
which lies buried in drifted sand, would have been the

largest in the world, and would have stood ninety-five feet in the column, and have been eleven feet square in the base.

Leaving the quarry, our thoughts full of the wonders of Egypt, we ride on over the arid sands through a stern and desolate defile, passing many a large stone building, on some of which are sculptured hiero-glyphics, the whole scene reminding you somewhat of the character of the Bab-el-Molouk in the Thebaid. At length the narrow defile opens, and you see before you the convent of the Austrian mission, and soon the river is reached, where boats are in readiness to convey you across to Philæ.

Philæ, which in Egyptian is Pileh, was so called from being the frontier between Egypt and Ethiopia. I had heard so much of the island and its beauty, that the first view disappointed me. I expected to see more verdure, more of that wealth of green which we are accustomed to associate with what is lovely in a landscape. But as you approach the little island, with its palms and its temples gleaming in the sun-light, and the deep shadows lying on the great purple rocks, its beauty grows upon you, and a little time spent on its shores is enough to make you captive to its charms. I spent some hours there on two occasions examining its temples, climbing its green mounds, and

ascending to its lofty pylon to look at the beautiful
view from the summit. On the west of Philæ is the
little island of Biggeh, rising amidst black and purple
rocks of fantastic shapes and grotesque forms.
Your eye is delighted by the yellow sands and the
sombre rocks, by the tranquil river and the encircling
hills, while your ear is soothed by the sound of the
cataract as it frets against the rocks a little distance
off. The island is soon traversed ; it is only about
400 yards long, and 140 broad. It is pleasant, after
a hot ride of some hours, to sit under the shadow of
the palms by the river, or within the cloisters of the
temples, and give yourself up to a waking dream of
the past glories of the lovely isle. The temples do
not take us back to the far-past days of the great
Pharaohs, the earliest name on the monuments being
that of Nectanebo II., an Egyptian prince who revolted
against the later Persian kings. ˙ He built the little
temple at the south end of the island, where is a chapel
dedicated to Isis. The other names found on the
monuments are those of the Grecian Ptolemies, and
of these the chief is Ptolemy Physcon, or " the fat,"
so called, as Dean Stanley reminds us, " because
he became so bloated by luxurious living that he
measured six feet round, and who proposed, but in
vain, to Cornelia, the mother of the Gracchi." A

large temple to Isis, distinguished by its unsymmetrical arrangement, also adorns the island. Of this Sir J. Fergusson says that "it contains all the play of light and shade, all the variety of Gothic art, with the massiveness and grandeur of the Egyptian style ; and as it is still tolerably entire, and retains much of its colour, there is no building out of Thebes that gives so favourable an impression of Egyptian art as this." "The ten-columned hall" is worthy of note. Here the colours are remarkably bright and fresh ; the ceiling is bright with a blue tint from which shine out stars in gold ; and the capitals are of the most vivid azure and green, with crimson and orange lines. Here, among other astronomical subjects, is the globe, with its widespread, all-embracing wings of blue, considered by some as an impressive type of monotheism, and suggestive of the sublime thought : "Under the shadow of Thy wings shall be my refuge." As this temple is dedicated to Isis, we find, as might be expected, many sculptures of this goddess, and Osiris, and Horus. In a small chamber there is a representation of the death of Osiris, his embalmment, burial, his resurrection, and enthronement as judge of the dead. In the court, with ten gigantic columns, there is a cross, and some other marks, such as an apse towards the east, which prove that this part of the temple was in the early Christian centuries turned into a Christian church. The Copts dedicated it to St. Stephen ; and "this good work," says a Greek inscription, "was done by the well-beloved of God, the Abbot, Bishop Theodore." There are other Christian records, such as, " The Cross has conquered, and will ever conquer ;" and some signatures—" I, Joseph," in one place, and " I, Theodosius of Nubia," in another. But the little basilica no longer resounds to Christian hymns, and Christian prayers are no longer offered in the sanctuary ; here the worship of Isis was supplanted by the Cross, the Cross has now been supplemented by the Crescent.

There is another lovely little temple at the east end of the island, oblong, rectangular, having a quadrangle of fourteen columns, to which no description can do justice, and which must be seen to be appreciated, commonly known as " Pharaoh's Bed." It is singularly elegant and graceful, open to the blue sky, and with no sculptures on its walls save one of the sun with widespread wings. There is great interest attached to Philæ, independently of its natural beauty, and the architecture and sculpture of its temples, from its being called " the Holy Island," as it shared with Abydos the fame of being the burial-place of Osiris. So sacred was it considered, that none might set foot upon its shores, or even approach them too closely without permission. The most solemn oath which an Egyptian could take was this : " By him who sleeps in Philæ." The story of Osiris is one of the most interesting of the Egyptian sacred myths. He ruled the world wisely, constituted laws, taught agriculture, and civilized Egypt. On his return from his travels over the world, his evil brother, Typhon, played him false, for he had a chest made of the exact length of Osiris, and offered it as a gift to any one whom it would fit. A feast was given, and all the guests tried the chest; and when Osiris lay down in it, the lid was closed, fastened down, and the chest thrown into the Nile. Then Isis, clad in mourning garments, searched for her husband up and down the earth, and found the chest, which had been cast up from the sea, at Byblon in Syria. While she was absent, Typhon again possessed himself of the body, and cutting it into fourteen pieces, scattered them over the land of Egypt. The widowed queen searched diligently for the scattered limbs, and whenever she found one, buried it in the place where it was discovered, and each burial-place was known as a grave of Osiris. The head was buried at Abydos. Osiris, returning from the dead, sent Horus, his son, to do battle with Typhon ; Horus was victorious over the

murderer of his father, and binding Typhon in chains
handed him over to Isis. Osiris now reigned with
Isis once more in the upper world. There is a meaning underlying this, as all other sacred myths. In
it we have the figure of the setting and rising of
the sun. The conflict between Osiris and Typhon
symbolizes the struggle between light and darkness,
life and death. We also trace in the resurrection of
Osiris a type of the immortality of the soul. In this
doctrine, as we have seen, the ancient Egyptian fully
believed, and he saw in the resurrection of his god a
symbol of his own triumph over death and the grave.

CHAPTER XX.

On Board the *Seti.*—In Nubia.—Scenery on Banks of the River.—Dress of the Natives.—Articles for Sale.—Village of Dabod.—Gorge of Kalabsheh.—The Bayt-el-Welly Temple.—Sculptures.—Amusements on Board.—A Disagreeable Fellow-Traveller.—Dendoor.

IT is with regret that one leaves Philæ, with its palm trees and temples, its beautiful outlook on granite rock, and silver stream, and dark purple hills, that form a background to the picture. As I and my party were about to go as far as the Second Cataract, we left the lovely island on our first visit with the less sorrow, because we knew we should pause there again on our passage down the Nile. We crossed the river in a ferry boat, and embarked on the *Seti*, a small steamer suited to the narrow channel of the river, and with accommodation for twenty-eight passengers. Only twenty-six were on board, and four of these were of my party. We were in Egypt no longer, but in Nubia. The water is clearer, the hills

rise more abruptly on each side of the river, and the
green corn and the blue flowering lupins come down
to the very edge of the stream. Sometimes a group
of date-palms or of Dôm palms meets the eye, and a
row of castor-oil trees fringes the edge of the river ;
and behind, dark granite or yellow sandstone hills
close in the scene, and the wild desert forms an arid
background. Water-wheels, which are numerous all
along the bank, are here more frequently turned by
oxen than men, for we are within the tropics, and the
sun has more power than lower down the Nile ; and
as the need of water is great, the monotonous, melancholy sound of the sakieh never ceases, night or day.
There are few villages, and the population is small.
The costume of the men who work among the beans,
and of the younger women who carry their naked
children slung round their necks, is of the scantiest.
Black as ebony are men, women, and children. The
hair of the fair sex, if so they can be called here, is
plaited into a hundred tiny curls, after being well
soaked with castor oil. It is usual to rub the body
with castor oil till it shines, for it affords protection
from the burning rays of a tropical sun. Yet these
" Berbers," as they are called, have pleasant faces,
and seem bright and good-humoured. Some of the
women are tattooed, and have blue lines on their

under lip, and on cheek and arm. They wear earrings and nose-rings, bead necklaces and large silver
bracelets. The elder women wear the usual long
blue garments, which they gather round them in folds;
but the girls, no doubt thinking that "beauty, when
unadorned, is adorned the most," simply wear the
leathern girdle, sometimes decorated with a fringe of
shells, round their loins.

When the boat stopped at any place where we were
to land, that we might see some place of interest, the
women would bring baskets or mats, strong and good,
and woven of different colours, and offer them for
sale, and they generally found some customers for
their wares. Sometimes they had live pigeons or
eggs ; sometimes glass beads, or a scarab which they
declared to be a veritable antique. They are good
at bargaining, and know the value of money. As
we passed up the river, we glided by many a temple,
close to the river's side, or not far from the bank, and
by some ruin which carried the thoughts back to the
past, when the fortress was built by some Ethiopian
king long gathered to his fathers. So we sail by the
small village of Dabod, on the western side of the
river, which widens here, and where are the ruins of
a temple begun by King Ashir-Amen, "the ever-
living." Its three pylons stand out clear from their

platform of sand. Then we come upon Gertrasseh, with its limestone quarries, and another small ruined temple standing on a cliff; and Tafa, with its clusters of palms; and anon we enter on a scene of wild beauty and grandeur, and pass, through El-Bab, "the gate," and through a series of rapids formed by dark purple rocks, into the fine gorge of Kalabsheh, lighted up by the midday sun. The gorge of Kalabsheh appeared to me much more beautiful and striking on our return down the river, than it did in ascending the Nile; the cliffs, the islands, the rapids were then seen to greater advantage. The day of our passage up the stream was cloudy; but there was a soft light upon the landscape, and pleasant it was to sit on deck, and watch the current of the river, broken into channels by great boulders of basalt, or by small islands covered with the very greenest of verdure. At Kalabsheh are the ruins of the largest temple in Nubia, but one comparatively modern, being of the date of Augustus, though it would appear that the stones of which it is built belonged to some older edifice, as the name of Thothmes III. may be traced on a granite statue before the entrance. But a far more interesting temple is the Bayt-el-Welly, "the house of the saint," which is within a mile of Kalabsheh, and cut out of the rock, and finely situated on a cliff, commanding a view of the river, and the green banks that shut it in. It is a small rock temple, with an adytum, and an inner hall, supported by two pillars, and is dedicated to Ammon-Ra, the supreme god. Here we meet the great Rameses again. He is represented as victorious over the Ethiopians, whose king and his children are captives in the hand of the conqueror's son ; and offerings of gold and leopards' skins, and oxen and gazelles, of apes and giraffes, are made to the victorious Pharaoh. On one side of the entrance court, the king is seen laying siege to the city of the Shori, and he is also represented in single combat with a chief of that nation. The sculptures are life-like, and the colours are generally fresh-looking and bright. After inspecting the paintings and sculptures of the temple, we returned to the boat, which anchored at Kalabsheh for the night, feeling some pleasure in the thought that we should be soon within the Tropic of Cancer. The evening was fine, the clouds dispersed, and the night was bright with stars. Orion was in full splendour, and Venus like a moon. The sky was of a deep purple, and the air soft and still. It was the night of the 16th of January, and one could not help contrasting the climate in Nubia with the weather in mid-winter in England. We had exchanged the snow and the frosts,

and the harsh winds of which our letters spake, for
the deliciously mild air on the banks of the Nile. We
had a pleasant party on board, most of them English,
but some American. There was a good piano in the
saloon, and when it grew dark, or when we grew tired
of sitting on deck, we gathered round the instrument
to listen to the music, or to read, or write up our
journals, or play a game of chess or draughts. The
doctor on board had a sweet voice and much taste,
and some ladies of the party sang and played well ;
so that with music, and conversation, and reading, the
evenings in the *Seti* passed very agreeably indeed.
One of the enjoyments of travelling is the meeting
with pleasant people ; and I must say we were very
fortunate in our fellow-passengers on the Nile, some
of them highly cultured and of wide reading, in whose
society time went not only lightly but profitably.
There were scientific men, and men of travel ; ladies
who sketched admirably, and had a true feeling for
art ; and a gentleman whose friendship was a
privilege, a former governor of the State of Michigan,
and a senator of the United States. There are
Americans *and* Americans, as there are Englishmen
and Englishmen ; and it was a pleasure to meet and
to become acquainted with very many of those who
had come across the Atlantic. Why some Ameri-

cans travel it is difficult to say, their great object seeming to be to hurry from place to place, and not to give time enough to see any one place well. One gentleman made a boast of seeing and doing many countries in a short time, and when speaking to a friend of mine of the lands he had visited, said that he had seen all Europe, and had "just gone through it like a dose of salts." A lady from the same country, who was travelling alone, expressed herself "tired of the whole thing," and hated temples and tombs, and while the rest of us were busy exploring the wonders of the shore, remained on the boat reading a novel, or gazing listlessly before her. She was never weary of expressing her disgust with the country and the people, and contrasting them with her own country and people, much to the advantage of the latter and the disadvantage of the former. She was disagreeably aggressive both in the matter of politics and religion, and would again and again wish herself in her own country—a wish which was devoutly echoed by us all. Her fellow-countrymen begged of us somewhat piteously not to take her as an example of Americans.

Some Americans must delight in perpetual motion. I heard on good authority from a countryman of his, of one gentleman who lives on the railway between

New York and Chicago, eats, drinks, and sleeps, and
transacts all his business in the train.   He never
leaves his carriage, but makes it his home.

On Tuesday, the 17th of January, we left Kalabsheh
early in the morning, with the melancholy sound of
the shadoof in our ears.   It had been droning and
creaking during the night, and its moaning seemed
to mingle with our dreams.   In a short time we
entered the Tropic of Cancer, and so passing quietly
along reached Dendoor, where there is a pylon and
a small temple of the Roman period, dedicated to
Osiris, Isis, and Horus.   The people of the village
crowded round us, begging us to buy their wares—
the usual necklaces, and beads, and bracelets—and
clamouring for backsheesh.   The scenery is wild
and stern, relieved only by the bright green of the
river bank, and the silver windings of the Nile.   Some
purple hills rise in the distance, and the sand is
literally golden, bright and beautiful, and of a colour
more lovely than I had yet seen.   I understood, as
I had not done up till now, the meaning of the phrase
"golden sands."

The walk to Dendoor was taken before breakfast,
for which it had given us an appetite on our return
to the *Seti.*   The Nile now increases in breadth, and
the scenery assumes a new and singular character.

From the vast Libyan desert rise isolated volcanic peaks of a pyramidal form. The cones vary in height and size ; some are circular and low, others rise up in great purple masses against the blue. They lend a new and interesting character to the landscape, and give the traveller the idea that he is journeying through a land of pyramids.

CHAPTER XXI

WE now reach Dakkeh, where are the remains of a temple built in the time of the Ptolemies. Its sculptures and hieroglyphics show traces of different builders, but perhaps its chief interest lies in the history of the Ethiopian king, Ergamum, who lived about 50 years B.C., and who resolved to break through the custom which ruled the length of a royal reign in Ethiopia. Hitherto the priests had intimated to the king that the gods now wished him to enter their presence, and that the time had come when he must die. The king resigned himself to the wishes of the gods, and put an end to his existence without a murmur. Ergamum had the courage to do away with this custom. Not waiting for the summons from the oracle, he gathered his troops, and marching to the temple, slew the priests, and reformed some of the old institutions. Sir Gardner Wilkinson, in his *Modern Egypt and Thebes*, points out the fact that a similar custom still lingers in some parts of Ethiopia, where it is thought disgraceful that a king should die a natural death from disease or old age ; and so, when one of their sovereigns is about to die, he sends word to his ministers, who immediately cause him to be strangled. Though Ergamum refused to believe the priests when they declared the will of the gods as to his death, he honoured the gods themselves, as is seen in his temple, where he is represented as making the usual offerings to the deities, and where he receives from them in return a stream of the symbol of life, poured from two vases which Ra and Thoth hold in their hands.

After examining Dakkeh, and ascending a winding stair of sixty-five steps, to see the top of the propylon, in order to get a view of the desert and the Nile, we returned to the boat, and sailing past the ruins of Maharrakah, did not stop again until we reached the Wady Sabooa, "the valley of the lions," so called from the avenue of sphinxes which led up to the propylon in front of the temple. The temple of the great Rameses is but a short way from the shore, and is almost buried in the golden sand. The sphinxes too, are more or less embedded in the sand, and the features of the two that are best seen are nearly defaced. One huge head lifts itself above the sand, and the calmness of its countenance, as it seems to gaze in mournful majesty on its buried brothers, is most impressive. Two rude colossal statues of Rameses, on which are sculptures proclaiming his wars and his victories, stand at the entrance of the dromos. Within the gateway of the temple there is a hall divided into three aisles by ten Osiride figures, which support the architrave, five being ranged on each side.

Again we were beset by men, and women, and children from the neighbouring villages, who brought the usual wares for sale ; and one of the ladies of my party bought a musical instrument made of straw, called a tabourra, from a small boy as black as Erebus.

The boat "tied up" for the night, and in the early morning left for Korosko ; and as we sailed up the river we saw that the Nile made a considerable curve, and that in the distance were ranges of barren hills extending towards the horizon, and that the foreground was made beautiful by the feathery palm and the graceful mimosa. We were now full of hope of seeing a crocodile, but none came up from his river

bed to give us this satisfaction; and, indeed, the crocodile is now being driven farther and farther up the
Nile by the steamboats, and it is thought that in a
little while he will disappear altogether from this part
of Egypt. Besides, the weather was not warm enough
to attract him to some sandbank, that he might bask
in the sun; indeed, the day was cloudy and chilly, and
when we reached Korosko it rained heavily. We were
sorry to sail past this, the chief town of the province,
without going on shore, for we knew that here lay the
caravan road across the desert to Berber; and that
by this road General Gordon went to Khartoum in
1884. We had the promise, however, of stopping at
Korosko on our way down the Nile, and so we
believed our landing there only a hope deferred.
Alas! hopes are not always fulfilled. It continued
to rain very heavily—a most unusual thing, we were
told, in this climate; such rain had not been known
for ten years; and when we reached Derr, passing
Amada with its little temple on the way, the rain
had not ceased, and we opened our umbrellas for the
first time since our arrival in Egypt. It was very
disappointing, but we could only make the best of it,
and hope that the clouds would soon break, and the
sun and the blue sky appear. We hoped against
hope. The rain was like the rain in Westmoreland,

where they say, "it never rains; it always pours."
We were resolved, however, to see the capital of
Nubia, and so walked bravely forth to the mud
village, to see the temple which stands behind the
Mudir's, or governor's, house.   It was the only temple
we saw in Nubia on the eastern bank of the Nile.
The governor's house was of mud, with a coping of
bricks round the top, and the entrance is through a
gateway of stone.   The governor came out to meet
us, received us hospitably, offered us coffee, and in
return we gave his excellency—what he evidently
expected—"backsheesh," and he received it with
gratitude.   He was an old man descended from the
Kashefs of Sultan Selim, a family which had long
been governors of the province, but which had been
deprived of its authority by Mohammed Ali.   The
people of the village, however, who are proud of
their Turkish descent and their light complexion,
still regarded him with respect on account of an
ancestry dating from time immemorial, and would
have preferred his rule to that of a stranger.   But
" the old order changes " in Nubia as elsewhere.

The temple lies beyond the old governor's house,
and is little else than a ruin.   It dates from the time
of Rameses the Great ; and here, on pillar and wall
and doorway, the king is seen in bas-relief, making

offerings to Ammon-Ra, and the walls are covered with hieroglyphics. Among the sculptures we see the king and his captives, his children and his lion. Above the lion is an inscription which Champollion translates thus : " The lion, servant of his majesty, tearing his enemies to pieces " ; and Champollion discovered here a list of the sons and daughters of the king, there being seven sons and eight daughters, placed according to their age and rank, with a declaration of their names and titles. The temple looked gloomy, and the chambers had a dim and dreary appearance ; but this may have been the effect of the wet and dismal weather, and I was not sorry to leave the ruins, and proceed again to the boat. On a fine day I can imagine that Derr is not without beauty, for in the foreground there are groups of noble palms, tall and strong, with exquisite plumes—and the palm is always a beautiful object— and in the distance are long ranges of sandstone cliffs, which, when the sun shines, must gleam and glisten like gold. On the way back we were tempted by many articles offered for sale by the people : baskets and bowls made of the fibre of the palm, beads and necklaces, of which there seemed a plentiful supply. The only thing I bought here was a chameleon, the largest I had ever seen, and which was rescued from the hands of a boy, who had tied its tail tightly with a piece of string, which must have caused it great pain ; and I bore it with me to the ship, hoping it would live and thrive. It was a fine specimen, and changed its colour repeatedly, its black spots showing sharply against the green.

CHAPTER XXII.

THAT afternoon we reached Ibreem, 15 miles from Derr, and 142 miles from Philæ. The Nile has here become very broad, and large sandbanks divide it into narrow channels. The rain continued, but we went ashore, and climbed the great rock to see the ruins, and the splendid view from the summit. Ibreem, in the words of Miss Edwards, is "a sort of ruined Ehrenbreitstein on the top of a grand precipice overhanging the river," and was a station of some importance in the time of Candace, queen of the Ethiopians, when the Romans were in possession of Egypt and Nubia. Strabo tells us that the Queen Candace, who marched against Ibreem, the ancient "Primis Parva," was a contemporary of Augustus, a woman of masculine courage, and had lost an eye. Candace was the name of a dynasty,

just as " Pharaoh " was of the earlier, and "Ptolemy"
of the later kings of Egypt. The chief interest of the
fortress lies in the huge blocks of stone, which were
taken from ancient buildings, and used for the construction of the outer wall, for some of these bear
the name of Tirhakah, king of Ethiopia, who ruled
Egypt and his own country 700 years B.C. This is
the king that is mentioned in the 2nd Book of Kings
as reigning in Ethiopia at the time of Sennacherib's
expedition against Jerusalem. There are grottos in
the rock below Ibreem, and these, it is said, have
paintings inside, and here are to be read the names
of Thothmes I. and III., of Amenhotep II., and of
Rameses II. ; but they are very difficult of access,
and can only be reached by a rope by which you are
drawn up, so we did not attempt an entrance.

On the morning of Thursday, January 19th, we left
Ibreem, and the weather was again cold and grey.
We were now full of hope and impatience. We were
steaming up towards Aboo Simbel, and the scenery
was constantly changing. The beautiful foliage of
the palm-tree was no longer seen ; volcanic peaks
again rose strangely weird in the distance ; the verdure on the river banks had shrunk to a narrow strip,
and the river flowed in many places through a desert.
But as if to compensate for this, the sands on the

western bank glistened like gold, and were a joy to look at. Presently the hills about Aboo Simbel come into view ; every eye is directed to the western bank ; every head is lifted to catch a first glimpse of the rock-cut temples, of which so much has been written and said, and every heart beats with excitement. At last the great temple becomes visible, cut out of the massive rock, with the four gigantic statues facing obliquely eastwards, and looking across the river to the vast desert beyond; and here Rameses II., the glory and honour of his times, is seated in awful tranquility and repose. For centuries he has sat here, unchanged amidst change, while dynasties have fallen, and thrones tottered to their fall. We see, as we slowly pass, that these colossal sentinels, with their faces to the sunrise, sit two on the right side and two on the left of the entrance to the temple, their hands resting on their knees, and their feet a little asunder. A too hasty glance at the wonders of the façade of the great temple of Ipsambul, and then the smaller temple of Hathor, "the Lady of Aboshek," comes into view, and forms a very striking object from the river. There are six statues cut out of the rock, standing thirty feet high, three to the right and three to the left of the entrance to the temple, and they represent Rameses and Nofreari, his queen. Nofreari appears under the form of the goddess Hathor, and on her head she has the crown. of the goddess—the moon contained within the horns of a cow—and she wears also the ostrich feathers, which are the insignia of royalty. Their children are beside them, her daughters close to the queen, his sons near to the king, and these infants measure ten feet in height. But when we return from Wady Halfa we shall have time to examine the statues and temples of Aboo Simbel, to enter its solemn courts, and inspect the scenes of war and triumph depicted on its walls. I would fain have landed there and then, and seen the glories of the great temple of the great Rameses, and the "divine abode" which the hieroglyphs on the outer wall of the smaller temple tell us "was made by Rameses, the Strong in Faith, the Beloved of Ammon, for his royal wife Nofreari, whom he loves." I had to school my mind to patience, for I had just been reading, in *A Thousand Miles up the Nile*, how the legend within the door-way of this same temple, records, after enumerating the titles of the king, that "his royal wife, who loves him, Nofreari, the Beloved of Maut, constructed for him this abode in the mountain of the Pure Waters." Here, then, in these desert places was the spirit of poetry and romance ; here, in the ages gone by, the old, old story—old, but ever new—had been retold ; and, in the words of Miss Edwards, "we feel that Love once passed this way, and that the ground is still hallowed where he trod."

CHAPTER XXIII.

THE day still lacked the brightness we looked for in the tropics ; and the burning blue of the sky, and the luminous air, and the amethystine glow on the hills that we had read of, were on this morning things to be desired and not realized.   As we sat on deck in our overcoats and wraps, we passed long ranges of mountains, evidently volcanic, black in colour and fantastic in shape.   These rise on the western bank of the river, and are seen for some miles above Aboo Simbel ; and then the chain terminates, the river is divided, a little farther up, into two branches, by a large island crowned with palms, and hills with conical peaks loom up in a weird fashion on both sides of the Nile.   The day was cold and grey, but

it was calm, and the wind from the north was favourable, and neither keen nor cutting. Travellers say
that there is usually a strong wind, sometimes rising
into a gale, near Wady Halfa ; but this was not our
experience on the 19th of January, 1888 ; and we
passed rapidly but quietly up the river, till the *Seti*
anchored under the green palm trees of the Southern
Frontier. It was the eve of the Mohammedan Sab-
bath, and the river was full of men bathing and wash-
ing themselves in anticipation of the sacred Friday.
They were in no sense disconcerted by the approach
of the *Seti*, and pursued their pleasant occupation
with the greatest unconcern. It was early in the
afternoon, and so we went on shore at once, wishing
to see what we could of the frontier, and to visit
a place whose name had become so familiar in the
Egyptian war. I carried a letter of introduction
from the general in command at Cairo, General
Dormer, to Colonel Chermside, who was in command at Wady Halfa. There is nothing now of
interest to be seen at the frontier, save the camp and
the cataract, for all that remains of the three temples
that once stood here are a few broken pillars and part
of a ruined brick pylon. There are some palms close
to the landing-place, and one large tent used by the
English officers is pitched under the shade of a fine

old sycamore-tree. Four thousand Egyptian troops
are stationed here, and fifteen English officers are in
command. Colonel Chermside took us over the com-
modious cavalry stables ; and under the guidance of
another officer we saw the Camel Corps at its exercise.
The weather was so chilly, far south as we were—nearly
one thousand miles from Cairo—that as we went into
one of the officer's picturesque tents to rest, it was
more than pleasant to see a large fire blazing on the
hearth. The next morning was, however, more cheering ; the sun shone in a clear sky, and we started in
good spirits under the guidance of several of the
officers for the Second Cataract, who brought two of
their own camels for two ladies of my party who preferred to ride to Fort Kormūsa rather than go by
train. The railway that was constructed for the use
of the troops sent under the command of Lord
Wolseley in the autumn of 1884, to relieve General
Gordon in Khartoum, is still in use. The length of
the line is four miles and a half, and this distance our
camel-riders did in forty minutes, arriving at Kormūsa just before the train. We had hoped to go as
far as the Rock of Abooséer, from which the best view
of the cataract is to be had ; but it was not considered
safe to go so far, as the Dervishes were giving
trouble, and their scouts had been seen taking obser-

vations. We were permitted, however, to go to the English fort on the opposite side of the river ; and having been rowed across in one of the boats that, under the direction of Colonel Butler, had been built for the Nile expedition, and sent out from England, we landed at the foot of a steep cliff, up which we climbed to get the fine prospect which the eye takes in from the top. Though the view cannot equal that from Abooséer, yet it is worth seeing. A great part of the cataract is within sight, with its narrow channels, its black rocks, against which the waters foam and fret, its islets shining in the sun, and the purple hills and green palms which form the boundary of the view to the south. To the east stretched a sandy wilderness, on the nearest verge of which was a group of trees shadowing the mud houses of a village. Just across, on this western side of the river, was the Soudan ; and the camel-riders, on their return, rode a little way over the frontier, for the pleasure of saying they had been in that now famous territory. Far on the horizon two mountains were seen which mark the route to Dongola. Wady Halfa, if not classic, is historic ground ; and though it was a pleasure to visit this, the extreme southern frontier, the pleasure was mingled with regret when we remembered that the expedition, sent here as the base of operations to

P

relieve General Gordon, was all too late to save the life of that noble and heroic man. The policy of the Government was a policy of hesitation, and the tragical fate of Gordon was the result. The Ministry would not be convinced of the danger of the man whom they sent to the Soudan, so Khartoum fell, and the honour of England suffered by Gordon's death. I had the gratification of shaking hands with a fine-looking fellow, a Kurd, who had been with Gordon at Khartoum, and received a gold medal from his hands, which he showed with justifiable pride.

We left Wady Halfa on the afternoon of Friday, and the *Seti*, having a strong current in its favour, steamed by the sandhills on either side of the river; —past a straggling Dôm palm here and there, with its bifurcated branches ; past many a sandbank, and the pyramidal mountains which lift their peaks over the desert plain, and rise on the edge of the far horizon. We had sunshine now, and were on the look-out for crocodiles, but none as yet condescended to appear, and we bore the disappointment with all the stoicism we could summon to our aid. The chameleon seemed happy and at home in a little biscuit-box, and amused itself, when placed in the sun, by shooting out its tongue and transfixing some heedless sportive fly, which it swallowed with evident enjoyment. It was curious to watch the chameleon when he had marked his victim :—the stealthy approach,—the pause while his revolving eyes were fastened on the unconscious insect,—the lightning dart of his tongue, the tip charged with a viscous matter, which at once secured his prey,—and then the rapid transference of the poor little fly to his mouth. When I could not procure him any flies, he was given a little finely chopped meat ; but this he evidently considered but a poor substitute for his natural food. We reached Aboo Simbel early in the afternoon, and at once landed, and made our way to the temples we longed so much to see. We thought it best to visit the smaller one first, that it might not be in any way · dwarfed by comparison with its more colossal neighbour. This temple, dedicated to Hathor, " the Lady of Aboshck," has a façade ninety feet in length, containing six recesses, in each of which there is a colossal statue representing Rameses II., and Nofreari, his queen. Three of these figures, as has been said, stand to the right of the doorway, and three to the left, and are each thirty feet high. It has been already mentioned that the hieroglyphs on the front and sides of the portico tell the story of the building, and record the mutual and unspeakable love which existed between the great king and his fair and beautiful wife — the word "Nofri" meaning both beautiful and good. We entered the temple, which extends about ninety feet into the rock, and contains the shrine of the goddess Hathor, "the supreme type of divine maternity," to whom this temple was primarily dedicated, and who is represented by Queen Nofreari, who, adorned with the emblems of the goddess, appears on the façade as the mother of six children. The face of the goddess is characterized by mildness, sweetness, and grace.

Having examined the smaller temple, we turned towards the larger, full of desire to get near the great Colossi, the four awful sentinels hewn out of the rock, who have kept watch and ward at its portals for three or four thousand years. We knew them well from engravings and photographs, and by description, but to be appreciated they must be seen. We climbed up the cataract of golden sand which leads to their feet, and to the doorway of the temple, and stood looking at the four portrait figures of Rameses II. for some time. They sit sixty feet high without the pedestal; and we learn from Murray that "the ear measures three feet five inches; fore-finger (*i.e.*, to the fork of middle finger), three feet; from inner side of the elbow-joint to end of middle finger, fifteen feet." The figure to the south is the most perfect, and has a face of much sweetness ; the expression is calm and placid. The head of one of the statues is broken off, and lies buried in the sand; the other two are tolerably perfect, but one has lost his beard, and both of the arms are gone. Notwithstanding the hard rock from which they are hewn, and the immense size of the features, the expression of the mouth and the curves of the nostrils are as delicately wrought as if they were moulded in marble or in clay. Certainly the old Egyptians handled their material with masterly facility, and understood the nice and difficult art of rendering character and expression in the face. They evinced not only much skill, but great artistic excellence in their sculptures.

The statues are naked to the waist, and on their heads is the crown of Upper and Lower Egypt, round their necks is a collar cut in relief, and high on each arm is the royal cartouche. The legs and feet are in proportion to the immense size of the body, and the limbs of the shattered Colossus are covered with inscriptions. On the left leg of this statue is the famous Greek inscription, dating from the reign of Psammetichus I., and cut there, just as modern travellers cut their insignificant names on rocks and statues now, and deface them by their tasteless scrawls. However, in this instance, we are deeply grateful to the soldiers Damearchon, the son of Amabichus, and Pelephus Pelekos, the son of Udamus, for cutting their names and their mission as they passed this way with the king's troops in pursuit of the 240,000 Egyptians who, Herodotus relates, deserted because they were kept in garrison at Syene for three years without being relieved.[1]   Can it be that the Egyptian deserters numbered so many, or is this an exaggeration of the historian's?   This, and the other Greek inscriptions at Aboo Simbel, are " the oldest existing, " Murray tells us, "to which a date can be given, and have been of the greatest use in the study of the history of the Greek alphabet.   They were written in the 7th century B.C."   It cannot be said of many modern travellers who write their names, or cut their initials on temples or tombs, that they leave behind them a record which shall be of interest and use to the future historian.

---

[1] Herodotus, ii. 37.

CHAPTER XXIV.

THE temple, at whose portal sit the four colossal figures, as solemn and majestic warders, consists of an entrance hall, beyond which lies a second hall supported by four square pillars; and beyond this again, a transverse chamber, the walls of which are covered with bas-reliefs of the gods, and with paintings glowing with colour. Beyond is the sanctuary. Here sit four figures larger than life—gods of the temple, with their hands on their knees—Phtah; Ammon-Ra, the supreme god; Ra, a chief among gods; and Rameses, now a god; and before them is a broken altar, cut out of the solid rock. In the first hall are eight colossal figures, four ranged on each side. Each is crowned with the pschent, or royal head-dress. Their hands are crossed on their breast,

215

and they clasp the crook and scourge, which are
emblems of majesty and power. Though the attitude is the attitude of Osiris, the face, so familiar to
us, and so serene, is the face of Rameses the Great.
By the aid of candles, and a brighter light from the
magnesium wire, we were able to see something of
the battle scenes on the walls—the conquering
Egyptians, with their chariots and horses ; the vanquished enemy, and the prostrate victims. There is
a fortified town, and a siege ; from the mighty bow in
the king's hand speed the arrows that pierce his foes,
and the besieged are in such great straits that they
beg for mercy. Again, in another picture, the king is
seen returning in triumph, preceded by captives, some
Asiatics, some evidently negroes, for they are woolly-
headed, thick-lipped, and all are represented to the
life. In one picture the king, pitiless in his cruelty,
slays the captives, whom he grasps by their hair.
Farther on you see a procession of priests carrying
the sacred boat, which is borne on poles ; and farther
on still is the figure of the king presenting his offerings to the gods. But the glory of Rameses is the
theme of all the designs—Rameses, placid and gentle-
looking, even while he draws the sword and slays his
helpless foes.

When we look at these colossal statues of Rameses,

and think how he glorified himself, and built temples
to his honour, and placed himself there in the granite,
as if he were a god, and might be worshipped as such,
we call to mind the Pharaoh of the Bible, who could
say in his pride to Joseph, " I am Pharaoh," and by
whom Joseph swore, as if he could swear by no
greater, when he said to his brethren, " By the life of
Pharaoh ye shall not go forth hence, except your
youngest brother come hither."

I have given but a very meagre description of the
pictures and sculptures of this wonderful temple,
which demands days for the proper study of its
various chambers and courts. After we had wandered through its dark and silent chambers, it was
pleasant to come out into the sunlight, and see the
blue river gliding along, and the glistering sands
and the green banks, and the purple peaks in the
distance. We saw the temple with its wonderful
façade by the glowing light of the afternoon, by the
tender light of the evening, and the golden light
of the early morning ; and the Colossi, sitting there
majestic and placid, were, under all aspects and at all
times, solemnizing and impressive.

I did not see an effect which may be witnessed at
certain seasons of the year, and in the morning, as
the rising sun smites the façade of the temple. A

gentleman whom I met, and who ascended the Nile later in the spring, told me he had the great pleasure of seeing it. As the sun gradually appears above the hills, a shaft of light pierces through the narrow doorway, penetrates the great hall, illuminates the darkness, and sheds a brightness on the altar and the four divine figures that sit within the shrine. It is conjectured that this effect was calculated on, that so on the great festivals it might light up the dark recesses of the sanctuary, and reveal the hidden gods. This only happens twice in the year; only twice in the twelve months does the sun at his rising so face the great temple that he fills its chambers with his glory. Happy they who visit Aboo Simbel at the favoured season !

We also went into the small temple discovered by Mr. McCallum and Miss Edwards in February, 1874, and which Dr. Birch supposes to have been the library of the great temple of Aboo Simbel. The wall paintings, bearing the portraits of Rameses II., and the spaces covered with hieroglyphs and sculptures, are by no means so fresh or so bright as when the little monument was laid open. It is now difficult to make out the names of those who spent so much time and labour on uncovering the Speos, as they are partly effaced; but whether this is owing to the injurious effects of wind and weather, or to the destructive instincts of the tourist, is a matter for conjecture. The ignorant tourist and the persistent collector work more harm upon ancient monuments than do all the destructive forces of nature.

Close to the great temple and its four solemn sentinels, and at their feet, there is a small granite tomb, the last resting-place of a brave English officer, Major Tidswell. He died of fever on the Nile, and here all that was mortal of him was laid, on the river's bank and amid the golden sands. There was something pathetic in this lonely tomb, and in the thought of him who died so far from home and friends, and whose grave was made in this distant land, with none who loved him near. His friends may be assured that his tomb is thought of and cared for, and kept freed from the encroaching sand, by English officers quartered on the Nile, and by Englishmen who pass up and down the river.

We left Aboo Simbel about noon on Saturday, January 20th. The weather had become quite beautiful, warm and bright, and the sun shone in a sky of cloudless blue. Pleasant it was to glide with the current, with just the faintest ripple of a breeze, and to be borne past rock and sandbank, and distant hill, and near banks green with corn, past palms, and plantations of the castor-oil shrub, with a glow of beauty upon all. As the day was hot, we were full of hope that we should see a crocodile ; and, lo! as we sailed quietly along, and were approaching a sand-bank, the captain came with the intelligence that there was a huge creature basking high and dry in the sun. There was a general excitement. All rushed to the western side of the boat, and over there, on a bank of sand, lay what appeared to be a dark log of wood. "Where is the crocodile?" "Yonder," said the captain, pointing to the log. "You are jesting," was the reply ; "that is only the trunk of a tree ; it cannot be a crocodile." "We shall see," said he. Upon which he clapped his hands, and raised a shout ; the brown log moved, stirred, awoke from its happy slumber and pleasant dreams, and running down the sloping bank, disappeared quietly in the water. I never thought that a crocodile could run so swiftly, but had fancied they were slow in movement, and that they turned themselves round with difficulty ; but I believe these ideas must be remanded to the region of myths. I may say here that two more crocodiles were seen in our passage to Korosko, and that our desire to see these creatures, once the object of worship, was fully gratified,

TIDSWELL.

Where Aboo Simbel's giant temple stands,
  And carved in rock four noble forms appear,
  That thus have sat enthroned through many a year,
There lies just at their feet, 'mid golden sands,
A lonely tomb, the work of tender hands,
  Which keeps the dust of one, a stranger here,
  Who rests apart from all who hold him dear,
And weep his loss in the far English lands.

Surely I deem that all who hither come,
  Cast a sad look on that pathetic grave,
Which bears a name,—God knows how dear to some,—
  " Tidswell,"—true gentleman, and soldier brave,
Who now sleeps well beneath the sunlit dome,
  Close to the music of the Nile's dark wave.

ABOO SIMBEL.

O great Rameses on thy awful seat
  At Aboo Simbel, 'midst the golden sands,
  Who carried war's fierce torch to distant lands,
And trampled kingdoms 'neath thy conquering feet,
Upon whose brow Egypt's two crowns did meet ;
  Here in "the mountain of pure water" stands
  A house divine built by thy loving hands,
For her to thee above all women sweet.

Although so great, thou couldst be tender too,
  For in this carven figure at thy side,
Stands Nofreari, fair and gentle-eyed,
  Whom in her youthful beauty thou didst woo,
And made her all thine own, thy life, thy bride,
  And held her to thine heart as lovers do.

CHAPTER XXV.

A S we sailed onward, the *Sett* came upon a sandbank, and we were detained some time before she could be got off, so that when we reached Korosko it was half-past six o'clock, too late to land and climb the hill for a view, as it was quite dark. This was a disappointment; but so great had been our enjoyment, and there had been so much food for thought, that all murmuring was restrained. I was most anxious to see the Southern Cross before we left the tropics; and so I determined to make an effort that night to accomplish my wishes. On going to my berth, I resolved to get up at any hour I should awake, and look out to see if the constellation were visible. Such a resolution is sure to fulfil itself. I awoke about half-past two, and rose. The sky was clear and cloudless. The stars and constellations were brilliant—Jupiter, Venus, Orion, shining with a splendour unknown in more northern latitudes. I looked towards the east, and there, very low on the horizon, what I believe to be the Southern Cross was shining. Was I disappointed? Yes. It was far from being the brilliant constellation I thought it to be; but I was nevertheless glad to have seen it, and returned to my cabin with a wish that had been long cherished, now gratified and fulfilled.

The boat left Korosko about dawn, and bore us away to Philæ at the rate of about thirteen knots an hour. The morning of Sunday was beautiful, and we all assembled, as usual, in the large saloon for service, to which the piano had been moved that we might have an accompaniment to the singing of the chants and hymns. All was quiet till towards the middle of an address that I was giving, when suddenly there came a great shock, and it seemed as if the boat would heel right over. There was a pause, but no one moved; the ladies exercised much control; and the service, interrupted for the moment, was continued, and finished "decently and in order." We found that the *Seti* had again run upon a sandbank, and it was some time before she could be got off; but this was at length done, and she dropped smoothly down the current. There was a strong breeze from the north, and the Nile rippled and sparkled in the sunshine; and to the east the hills rose up purple to the blue sky. So we glided past Wady Sabooa, and Dakkeh, Gerf Hassayn, and Dendoor, and entered the fine gorge of Kalabsheh, looking far more beautiful than it did on our way up the river. It is a striking scene, with its islands and rapids, hemmed in by black and towering mountains, and offering, at every bend and curve of the Nile, which winds here like a snake, the most varied and picturesque views. I was sorry when we left it, and the great purple hills, and granite cliffs, and golden sands far behind us, passing from the tropics and climate out of Nubia, and came to anchor about four in the afternoon opposite Philæ, with its temples and palms.

We left the boat early the next morning, January 23rd, and crossed to the Holy Island, beautiful, full of memories of the past, where we again examined the sculptures and paintings, ascended the pylon, looked down upon the river, and heard the music of the distant cataract. How pleasant the sunshine, how warm the air, on this January day; and as we thought of the possible snows and frosts at home, and the raw and bitter cold, we wished that all whom we loved could be with us under the palms, or among the graceful columns of Pharaoh's bed. Friends were much in our thoughts, for we had received a packet of letters at Philæ, and had read them eagerly before we bade farewell to the *Seti.* It might have been June for the delicious warmth of the air ; and the little chameleon basked in the sun on a broken column, and caught the unwary flies for his amusement. " 'Tis a picture for remembrance." What pleasant hours we had that morning! Again we studied the bas-reliefs on the walls, the paintings on the ceilings, the lovely capitals of the pillars, the exquisitely carved lotus and papyrus, and the Hathor-headed columns of the great temple. There was beauty everywhere, and we have carried away an impression of it so deep as not to be readily effaced.

We left the Holy Island with regret, even though we had another pleasure in store—the shooting of the First Cataract, under the care of some English officers from Assouan, who had kindly come from Philæ to take us down the rapids. They had engaged boats, and the sheykh of the cataract to steer us safely through the narrow channels. After luncheon under the shade of the great temple colonnade, we took to the boat over which the sheykh himself presided, another boat following with the rest of the party ; and we were borne past masses of shining

Q

rock,—past huge blocks, and boulders of fantastic forms of a deep black colour, on many of which are carved cartouches and inscriptions. There are little islands in the shining water, covered with palms and tamarisks, and the banks of the river are green with acacias and gum-trees. We went steadily on with the current, and before we reached the rapids, turned aside to see one of the sights of the place. We left the boat to climb the steep bank, where we were surrounded by a crowd of almost naked men and boys, as black as ebony, who were ready to plunge into the most impetuous part of the stream—indeed, into the midst of the hurrying, rushing, tumultuous torrent—and swim down, and show us their agility and skill. And they did so. There was something wild in the scene. The men and boys, some on logs, some on rafts, some in small boats, with flags flying ; others, without any of these aids, but trusting to their powers of swimming, having leaped into the foaming cataract, were borne, now under the water, now upon the wave, safely down the torrent, and came up again, grinning, with triumphant looks. The whole thing was worth seeing, as giving us an idea of savage life. After they had claimed and had received backsheesh,—for it need not be said that in this country nothing is done without backsheesh—indeed, in what country, civilized or un-

civilized, is anything done without it? it is the ruling
power everywhere,—we re-entered our boat with the
sheykh and the Arabs of the cataract, and were rowed
to the scene of adventure. We passed through a
succession of little islets and granite rocks, and num-
berless eddies, and foaming whirlpools, and were skil-
fully steered through a labyrinth difficult to thread,
and which would have offered dangers to any but
experienced boatmen. It appeared as if at times the
small craft might be dashed against the rocks and
upset, or be whirled into the vortex of some treacherous rapid, or that we should be thrown headlong into
the strong current, to be borne along wheresoever the
waters pleased, or to be sucked down beneath the
surging wave. But we were under skilful guidance,
and so we got safely into smooth water without accident; and then the Arabs in our boat, which took the
lead in the adventure, challenged the boat that followed closely in our wake to a race, and every muscle
was strained, and every oar was vigorously plied, and
it was doubtful for some time which side would have
the honour of the victory. The men sang, and bent
all their energies to their work, the sheykh of the
cataract directing the Arabs in our boat; an increase
of backsheesh was promised by the English officers
if we should be the first to reach our destination; and

so, still keeping ahead, we were carried past the island of Elephantine, and with a run and a rush found ourselves at last under the Moorish ruin at Assouan.

NEAR KOROSKO.

The day is perfect, cool, and passing fair :
  The boat upon the river glideth calm,
  Past golden sands, green banks, and graceful palm ;
Such beauty is there in the earth and air,
As well might loose "the ravelled sleeve of care,"
  And shed upon the wounded spirit balm,
  Or strike the keynote of a holy psalm,
Or lift the soul to God in happy prayer.

To breathe at all this day is passing sweet,
  To gaze on earth, to look upon the sky.
The hours are winged with pinions all too fleet,
For lo, as if to make the joy complete,
  Two heavens are ours—one shining far on high,
One in the river flowing at our feet.

CHAPTER XXVI.

On Shore Again.—Sunset.—Cook, and Egyptian Tourists.—Life at Luxor.—Enjoyable Climate.—Loss of Chameleon.—Glorious Sunsets.—"The After-Glow."

THE steamer, the *Mohammed Ali*, was in the harbour waiting to receive us; and after an inspection of our cabins, I went on shore to have another look at the bazaars, and to make some further purchases of baskets, and whips, and knives of the country. I paid a visit to the American Mission Schools, which are here under a native teacher, and which are doing good work in the education of the young, the Scriptures being taught to all the children who attend. The English officers kindly brought a pretty little grey horse, which one of my daughters mounted, and under their escort she rode into the desert and saw the Besharine camp, and then had a gallop up to the fort, from which she had a splendid view of the setting sun. As seen also from the deck of the *Mohammed Ali*, the sunset was glorious. Such colours in earth, and air, and sky!

such a splendour on the Nile! The west was all aflame, and the gorgeous colours were reflected in the water, making a double glory : the heavens a roof of burnished gold, the waters a floor of amber and emerald and blue. And then the lights gradually faded, and the darkness came on, and the beauty passed away, only to be succeeded by beauty of another kind—by luminous stars that looked down with lustrous eyes, and filled the tranquil evening with their silver light. Some of the party got up early the next morning to visit the tombs recently discovered by Sir Richard Grenfell, before the steamboat left Assouan ; but as I had some hopes of returning to the frontier town of Egypt, and occupying a house, which one of the officers kindly placed at our disposal for a short time, I did not accompany them, and so lost the opportunity of seeing the tombs, which well repaid the effort of an early visit, and a somewhat steep climb to reach them.

We dropped anchor at Luxor the same evening, and in the morning left the *Mohammed Ali* for the Luxor Hotel, where, fortunately, we had secured rooms two months before, for there were many travellers, and some friends who had come down with us in the steamer were obliged to seek accommodation at a smaller hotel, the Karnak,

It was more than pleasant to settle down for some time at Luxor, where all was so full of interest, and where the climate was so delightful. During the five weeks I was there the weather was all that could be wished : cool mornings and evenings ; bright and sunny days ; a dry and balmy atmosphere ; and a January and February like a fine June in England. Where in Europe can there be found such a climate ? —little or no rain ; no keen or cutting winds ; no frosts or snows ; no winter ; a genial spring passing gradually into a beautiful summer. Egypt is becoming more and more a winter resort, and, thanks to the enterprise and energy of the Messrs. Cook, there is now every facility of visiting it with ease and comfort. This firm of managers, now so well known, and under whose conduct you may visit every quarter of the globe, has been often made a butt for laughter and mockery ; while those who have travelled under its guidance have been objects of banter, and have been ranked among "the Philistines ;" but this reproach is now fast disappearing, for princes and peers, church dignitaries and scholars, put themselves under its control, and all bear witness to the excellence of the management. Nubar Pasha told a friend of mine, in the course of conversation on the condition of the country, that he thought that Cook had been

onc of the greatest benefactors of Egypt ; for by his
energy and enterprise, the facilities he afforded for
travel, and the general excellence of his arrangements,
he had induced many to visit the country, and thus
had materially increased its welfare. The friend who
repeated to me these words of Nubar Pasha, is a
gentleman of position and influence ; and he quite
concurred in the opinion, and added that, in his
opinion, Egypt would more and more be visited, and
the banks of the Nile in a little time become as much
frequented as the Riviera. For those who are fairly
strong, and able to visit the wonders of the Thebaid,
Luxor offers delightful quarters, and affords ample
opportunities of studying Egyptian architecture and
Egyptian sculptures in the ruined temples on both
sides of the Nile, and in the wonderful sepulchres in
the valley of the Tombs of the Kings. There is a
pleasant garden attached to the Luxor Hotel, the
haunt of the hoopoe and the bee-eater, where you
always find shade in the warm hours of noon under
the shelter of the date palm, or beneath the branches
of the lebbekh acacia. There arc many trees in the
garden, among them the loofah tree, which bears a
long green pod, not unlike a large cucumber, and
which, when fully ripe, yields a vegetable sponge
which is much used. The cool shade afforded by the

sycamore fig or the mimosa was often very grateful, for on some days in February the thermometer stood at 95° in the shade. But I must say the climate was most enjoyable,—warmth by day, and coolness by night; and the life was far removed from hurry and bustle. With much to interest, and nothing to distract,—with companionship when you sought it in the saloon of the hotel, with quietness in your own room when quietness was desired,—the life at Luxor was as pleasant as possible. The pleasure of travel is much enhanced when you travel not alone, but bring part of your home circle with you, as in my case, to enjoy the health-giving climate and the wonders of the land. I feel sure the bright sunlight, and the balmy air, the dryness of the atmosphere, the quiet dreamy life, with enough of interest and occupation to preserve it from being monotonous, must be of the greatest advantage to one who suffers from an over-worked brain or from nervous depression. I owe much to the winter climate of the Nile, and can speak gratefully of the bright sunshine and bracing air, and of the beneficial effect it had upon one suffering from a feeble circulation connected with a weak action of the heart.

My chameleon had a fine time of it among the flies, which I must confess were a plague. I never saw such persistent flies. You could not drive them away; routed, they returned to the attack. They mocked at the keshaskhi, or fly-brush. Nothing daunted them ; and after you had made some extraordinary exertion to beat them off, they would, with the greatest assurance and nonchalance, settle down again upon your face or your fingers. It was a vain struggle ; the flies always came off victorious. The chameleon did what he could to lessen their number, and his little tongue drew many a one into his insatiable maw. But, alas ! his amiable efforts in this direction were soon to be lost. He was left for a few minutes one day on a sunny pillar in the garden—left all to himself—and when I returned to seek him, the place that knew him knew him no more. He was gone. Whether some bird made a sudden swoop and carried him off, or whether he simply made his escape among the trees and shrubs, I cannot say ; but to me he was lost for ever.

A pleasant time it was, that at Luxor ; always something to see, always something to do. ₁There was the temple of Luxor close at hand, at the very gates of the hotel, and Karnak two miles off, and the Theban valley across the river. What sunsets there were, and how beautiful the after-glow ! Evening after evening I used to walk through the garden to the raised parapet close to the entrance, from which the Theban valley and the Libyan hills are to be seen, behind which the flaming sun used to sink in splendour. The sky on such occasions was on fire. The horizon shone like gold. The Libyan hills became luminous with liquid violet, and amethyst, and rose. The sun gradually but rapidly set behind the barren range. Then all became sombre, and grey as an English twilight, and the colour faded and died away. So it continued for some ten or fifteen minutes. And then came the marvel of the afterglow. Did it descend from the heavens to the earth, or did it rise from the earth to the heavens? The sky and the river were again filled and flooded with light. The Nile was a mirror of molten gold, and crimson, and blue, with graduated tones of violet, and pink, and green. The feluccas on the stream, with their white lateen sails expanded like the wings of a bird, as they moved through all the splendours of the glow, looked like fairy boats on an enchanted river ; and the whole scene called to my mind the apostle's vision in the Apocalypse, when he saw " the sea of glass mingled with fire." What nights followed the sunset, and the dying away of the after-glow! The deep purple sky was a glory far and near. The moon washed the heavens and earth with her light. Venus shed down a soft yet brilliant lustre. One morning early, between three and four o'clock, I got up, and, looking out from a window that faced the east, I had the pleasure of seeing the Southern Cross very low down on the horizon ; but more brilliant still was Jupiter, and so clear was the air that I saw what I believe were his satellites with the naked eye. Was this possible ? There is a strange beauty in the skies in Egypt, from the hour when "the rosy fingers of the dawn" begin to paint the skies, to the cloudless sunrise, and onward through the sunlit day, to the last glimmer of light, when the sun is hidden behind the Libyan range, and in the soft stillness of the night,

> " The floor of heaven
> Is thick inlaid with patines of bright gold."

THE AFTER-GLOW.

The sun hastes to his setting once again,
    The western skies like molten jewels gleam,
    And splendour robes the hills, the palms, the stream,
And turns to gold the sandy level plain,
Where Thebes, "the hundred-gated," once held reign.
    And now he sinks—now fades the last pale beam,
    And all the glory passes like a dream
We long to keep, but long to keep in vain.

But see ! From out this grey and sombre sky,
    Like life from death, there springs a radiance new,

That with fresh beauty takes the ravished eye,
  A flood of amber, emerald, and blue ;
Dear God ! when sets my sun, oh, grant that I
  May leave such after-glow behind me too !

CHAPTER XXVII.

Opening of a Mummy-case.—Difficulty of Unrolling the Body.
— Herodotus on Embalming. — Painful Proceeding.—
Antiques.—Hotel Guests.—" Rameses II."

WHILE we were at Luxor, we saw a mummy-case opened, and the mummy unswathed. Some of the party on the *Rameses*, among them an Irish peer and his wife, went, under the auspices of the English consul, Ahmed Effendi, to the house of an Arab, who had possessed himself of several mummy-cases, and arranged with him that we should see one taken from its coffin and unrolled. We struck a bargain : if there were found with the mummy any amulets or scarabs, which were to become our property, the man was to have three guineas ; if nothing was found, he was only to receive one guinea. The case was painted with various colours, still fresh and bright ; the face was gilt, and some figures on the wood declared it to be 3,000 years old. We were full of anxiety and expectation, hoping for hidden treasure ; so the Arab, with the help of his men, proceeded to open the outer case. This done, the body, wrapped in cere-cloths, lay exposed to view. Then began the process of unrolling the body, and this was not a pleasant—nay, a painful spectacle. I had imagined that the mask had only to be gently removed from the face, and the garments to be easily unwound, but a hammer and gimlet had to be employed, and these were roughly driven into the mummy, and the folds of the linen were torn forcibly away. The difficulty of taking off the cere-cloths no doubt arises from the manner in which the body was embalmed. Herodotus tells us that when the embalmers, who have drawn out the brains through the nostrils with an iron hook, " have filled the body, from which the bowels have been removed, with pure myrrh pounded, and cassia, and other perfumes, frankincense excepted, they sew it up again ; and when they have done this they steep it in natrum, leaving it under it for seventy days—for a longer time than this it is not lawful to steep it. At the expiration of the seventy days they wash the corpse, and wrap the whole body in bandages of flaxen cloth, smearing it with gum, which the Egyptians commonly use instead of glue. After this the relations, having taken the body back again, make a wooden case in the shape of a

man, and having made it, they enclose the body ; and
thus, having fastened it up, they store it in a sepulchral chamber, setting it upright against the wall."

This process, " the steeping of the body in natrum,
and the smearing of the bandages of the flaxen cloth
with gum," makes it no easy matter to disengage
the cloths from the mummy. And this makes the unrolling of a body painful to witness. There is a want
of reverence about the whole proceeding. That poor
mummy was once dear to some one ; his sickness was
mourned over ; his death was lamented. He was
committed with tears to that wooden case ; friends
did all they could for him : had the most skilful
embalmer ; purchased a costly case ; placed the
sacred scarab, the precious amulet, with him in the
coffin, and buried the body in the sacred vaults.
And now you disinter that body, that has lain in its
sepulchre for 3,000 years, and in the roughest manner
you take off the garments of the grave, and expose
all that remains of it to the cold, unsympathising
eye of the stranger. Yes, so it is. I was glad when
the whole thing was over, and the mummy was
replaced in its coffin. Nothing was found in the case,
—some said it had been opened before ; and so the
Arab had to be satisfied with his guinea.

Luxor is known to be a place where not only

antiques are sold, but antiques are made.   There are men there who drive a thriving trade in forged scarabs and amulets, and figures of the gods in bronze and china ; and you are beset with men and boys who offer these things for sale, and declare them to be genuine and thousands of years old.   So well are many of these things made that it needs the practised eye of a connoisseur to detect the fraud, and it is expedient that the buyer should have a well-qualified opinion before he invests in a sacred beetle or a god. The three consuls stationed at Luxor keep in their consulates a variety of antiques for sale, and I believe they are to be trusted.   The German consul has a very good collection, from which I selected some that those learned in such matters have assured me are genuine.   There are also shops in the town where antiques found by the Arabs in the tombs and temples may be had ; and I have seen some beautiful alabaster vases, and scarabs for rings, and cornelian necklaces that were purchased from these dealers, who are very secret about their most valuable wares, only showing them to you when you are alone.   If it was known that they had such treasures, it might lead to awkward discoveries.   While I was at Luxor, M. Grebaut came from Cairo to superintend some excavations that were being carried on in the temple

R

there, in order to give employment to some of the
people who had suffered from the inundation of the
Nile, which had been unusually high the last year,
and had done much damage to the town and neighbourhood. M. Grebaut made a raid on the shops
where antiques were sold, and carried off to his
dahabeah all the treasures he could find, much to
the distress of the owners, for they had purchased
them from well-known seekers for hid treasure, and
they received no compensation for their loss. This
seemed somewhat hard, though doubtless the dealers
must have known that they were engaged in an
illegal trade. However, the houses of the consuls
were not entered, and they were permitted, for
obvious reasons, to retain their goods in peace. As
M. Grebaut was sent by the Government, the Boulák
Museum would be all the richer for his raid upon
the shops. We went with the English consul on
board the dahabeah, to which the discovered treasures
were conveyed ; and M. Grebaut, with great courtesy,
allowed us to see them all, and pointed out the most
valuable objects—mummy-cases, votive statuettes,
wood carvings, blue scarabs, and precious amulets—
and told us with grim satisfaction of the success
of his search among the dealers at Luxor, some of
whom were much the poorer since his arrival.

There were many pleasant people staying at the hotel, English and American, and some very agreeable Germans, all of whom contributed to make the days and evenings pass lightly and happily away. Many of them were highly cultured and intelligent, and took a deep interest in Egypt and its people. We made several excursions together, and found, when visiting the temples and tombs, the truth of the words : " Iron sharpeneth iron : so a man sharpeneth the countenance of his friend." Among the ladies were some good musicians, who enlivened the evenings with music, and added much to the pleasure of our Sunday services in the saloon, by their accompaniments on the piano to the chants and hymns. A clergyman from Ireland, who had come with his wife for the health of his son, had conducted the services for some months, much to the satisfaction of the visitors. We had a capital musician in a young man, classic in his taste, and who played Beethoven and Bach with great power of execution and admirable delicacy of touch. Not the least pleasant and cultured of the guests in the hotel was Canon Isaac Taylor, who has lately been known as the apologist of Mohammed and Mohammedanism—very mistakenly, I think—but who never obtruded his peculiar views upon this contested subject on others. I am indebted to him, among other things, for calling my attention to the fact of there being so little that is offensive in the Egyptian sculptures, and how in this respect they differ from the frescoes and bronzes, and other objects of art, which have been discovered at Herculaneum and Pompeii, and which reveal the social degradation into which those cities had fallen. We went together to visit one of the courts in the temple at Luxor, and he showed me how the exception proved the rule. He had formed a very favourable opinion of the tender conception which the old Egyptians had of their gods, and he pointed out some of the sculptures in the same temple which represent Ammon-Ra receiving the king, who brings offerings into his presence, when the god takes him by the hand, and fondles him, and shows him marks of affection and favour. So in other sculptures the king is seen seated among the gods, as already deified, nourished at their breast, folded in their arms, and admitted to intercourse the most familiar and free. But if all this is very beau. tiful, we must remember that it is the representation of the king's own idea of his greatness, and of a power belonging to him which is divine, and that it is he who thus pictures himself as such a favourite of the god, whose smile is attracted by his mighty and heroic deeds. For it is the apotheosis of Pharaoh by himself, He stands colossal in stature on the sculptured walls, while all others are dwarfed by his mighty presence. Some may be affected differently by these and similar representations ; but I confess that, as regards myself, these gigantic statues, these vast temples, with their pylons, and columned arches, and soaring obelisks, and avenues of sphinxes, are more awe-inspiring than winning, and they crush one with a sense of insignificance, and with the terrible power of the deity who is worshipped in the shrine. Turning from these symbols of awe and dread, a strange peace falls on the heart as we call to mind the revelation of Himself by One who makes Himself known as "the God and Father of our Lord Jesus Christ," and who leaves us not to conjecture what His character may be, but manifests Himself to us as "Love," through the incarnation of His only begotten Son.

RAMESES II.

Surely this man did deem himself a god,
  Was lifted up with superhuman pride,
  As one who was already deified.
His conquests he had carried far abroad,
And kings and peoples trembled at his nod ;
  And so he raised his statues far and wide,
  Constructed tombs to hold him when he died,
This great Colossus on the world who trod.

O vanity ! thy statues are o'erthrown,
 Thy palaces blocked up with drifting sand,
Thy tombs the owls and bats have made their own,
 And where thy temples once did proudly stand,
There now remains the shattered, prostrate stone,
 And ruin reigns triumphant o'er thy land.

CHAPTER XXVIII.

A S we wished to see Erment, its large sugar factory
and gardens,—the latter being more especially
my attraction,—we went in the morning by the express
steamer that was bound for Assouan, hoping to catch
another boat on its way down to Luxor in the evening. The morning was as bright and fresh as could
be desired, and the day just one for such an excursion.
Erment is the ancient Hermonthis, and not far from
the village are the ruins of an old temple long destroyed, which was built by the beautiful Cleopatra,
who sits with the little Cæsarion on her knees, and
who adores Basis, the sacred bull of Hermonthis. We
did not visit this temple, nor the ruins of a Christian church supposed to be built from its stones, but

247

being in an idle mood, we wandered under the sycamore trees which line the banks of the Nile, and turning away very soon from the sugar factory, sought
the large garden with its groves of orange and lemon,
and beds of roses. The dogs of Erment are described
by Herodotus, and the breed still exists. They are
rough-haired, savage beasts, uncertain in temper, and
not pleasant to come across when excited or angry.
They are attached to their masters, but do not take
readily to strangers. Dr. Lansing, of Cairo, has a
fine specimen of one of these dogs, presented to him
by a member of his church, who lives at Erment.
We spent some time in the garden under the shade
of the orange trees, and were allowed to gather the
fruit, and to pluck some roses, but not, of course,
without the usual backsheesh ; and then we took a
stroll through the bazaars, which are not important,
and after making a few purchases, walked to the river
to look out for the steamer which was to take us back
to Luxor. It was now five o'clock, and there were no
signs of the boat. We waited till the evening fell,
and the moon and stars lit up the deep blue sky,
and then we telegraphed to Esneh to know if the
steamer had arrived there, and had left for Erment.
The reply was that it had left Edfou, but had not
reached Esneh, and it was supposed to have run

into a sandbank. The news was not cheering; and being uncertain when it would arrive, we began to think of some means of getting back to Luxor, for Erment offered but poor accommodation for the night; and besides, friends at Luxor would be anxious on our behalf. While we were deliberating, a small private steam yacht came into the quay, and we began to hope that this might be placed at our disposal. Our dragoman went to see what could be done in this way, and asked the owner, a French engineer, whether it might be had. Meanwhile, the wife of the station-master,—for there is at Erment a railway connected with the sugar factory,—who lived in a house opposite the quay, and who had before this sent us out chairs, invited us into her house, which was most comfortably furnished, and there her husband soon joined us. They were Italians, and I cannot speak warmly enough of their courtesy and hospitality. They set before us oranges, figs, and biscuits, and the husband brought out two bottles of Vermuth, with goollehs of fresh water, and knowing that we had tasted nothing since mid-day on the steamer, pressed us to eat and drink. He would accept of nothing himself in return; nor would he allow his pretty children, in whose hands we wished to place some acknowledgment, to do so. He told

us that he was too glad to be of use to any one from
Europe. It was a pleasant experience, this, of kindly
human nature—pleasant to find one, far from his own
beautiful country, and on the strange banks of the
Nile, who evidently could enter so fully into the
meaning of the words, " It is more blessed to give
than to receive." Erment will ever have a place in
my memory from the hospitality shown to a somewhat large party by the Italian station-master in this
little town.

The French engineer placed his yacht at our disposal, but as it was not large enough to hold us all,
we also took a small boat, which, being attached to
the steam yacht, was towed quickly down the river.
It was a lovely night. The moon poured down a
flood of light, and many-coloured stars shone in the
cloudless sky. The air was soft and balmy, and there
was a vivid sense of enjoyment in gliding down the
river, past clusters of sycamores and groups of palms
silvered by the moon, to the haven where we would
be. We reached Luxor soon after nine o'clock, and
having given the sailors belonging to the steam yacht
a liberal backsheesh, we landed, and made our way to
the hotel. Not long after our arrival, the steamer that
we expected came in, having with some difficulty and
much delay been got off the sandbank into which it

had run. The Nile was now beginning to get low, and every day made a difference in its course through the Theban valley.

On the evening of January 27th, the night before the full moon and her total eclipse, we made a party, and rode out to Karnak to see the glorious temple by her light. It was a pleasant ride after the village was left behind, by corn-fields and bean-fields, under palms and acacias, all tipped with silver, to the massive pylons of El-Karnak. There we found the English consul with two gentlemen from Cairo, and joining them at their wish, Ahmed Effendi took us to the several points from which the curve and line of the columns could be best seen. The two red granite obelisks, the noble hall of columns, the beautiful clerestory, the vast walls, all looked most impressive and the very shadows seemed to glow as the moon lent her splendour to all. We climbed up one of the temple walls on the western side, and looked over the Theban valley, now as still and quiet as the Tombs of the Kings which were hidden behind the Libyan range. Three thousand years ago the same moon was lighting the valley as it was lighting it now, but where were those so full of busy life then?—where were the kings, and the nobles, and the priests,— the harper, with his harp,—the music, and the danc-

ing, and the fair girls with the lotus-flower wreathed
in their hair? We know much of that old life,
sculptured as it is on the temples and on the tombs;
and it all comes up before us now, with its pleasures and pursuits, with its laughter and its tears,
its wars and its conquests, as we stand on the wall
at Karnak and look out upon the city of the dead.
After some time spent amid the wonderful ruins, we
turned away in silence, and rode quietly home. The
total eclipse of the moon took place the next night,
the 28th of January, and all were anxious to see it in
the clear atmosphere of Egypt. It took place later
than in England, and it was some time after ten
o'clock that the shadow began to steal over the
moon's disc. The planet had a most weird appearance. The colour was chocolate, of a deep brown,
and had not the darker shade I have seen in a more
northern latitude. I cannot say what conception the
Arabs have of an eclipse, or if they know its cause;
but the whole village seemed excited, and they made
a circuit of the town several times, singing in their
own unmusical, monotonous manner, and beating their
musical instruments. I asked next day of a young
Copt what the meaning of their songs might be, and I
was told they were singing hymns to God. " Oh, my
Lord, look and see. Some of us are children, the

others are men. Pardon, O Lord. Do, O Lord ; we are Thy servants, O Lord." As far as I could make out, they had some superstitious feeling that the darkened moon was a sign that the end of all things was drawing near.

There is a small Copt church at Luxor, which I went to see, and found it both mean and dirty. A large number of the population is Coptic. The Copts are no longer, as formerly, confined to one peculiar quarter ; they live on a very friendly footing with their Mohammedan neighbours. The Copts are descended from the ancient Egyptians, and many trace a resemblance between them and the sculptured portraits on ancient temple walls. Their eyes are dark and almond-shaped, and they are generally small in stature. Their dress is much the same as that of the Moslems, but they wear a black or blue turban and kaftan, and these colours are never seen on the head of the former. Their doctrines, which are those of the sect known as Jacobites, so called from Jacobus Baradæus, a Syrian, who propagated the Eutychian heresy, were condemned by the Council of Chalcedon in the year A.D. 451. Their liturgy, based upon some old forms, is in the Coptic tongue; but as this has practically become a dead language, they translate it when read, and the lessons from the Bible, into Arabic, for the

benefit of the people. Indeed, it is said that the
priests themselves know nothing of the language.
The services are very long, lasting from 7 a.m. to 10
a.m. They have tawdry pictures in their churches, and
sometimes figures of the Virgin and Child, and the
Saints ; and these material representations of holy
persons and things are a great stumbling-block to the
Moslem, who regards them as idols ; and their saint-
worship stands in the way of his reception of Christianity. I believe there is no greater hindrance to the
progress of Christianity in the East than the superstitious creed, and the idolatrous ritual of the Latin, and
Greek, and Coptic Churches. They raise an almost
insurmountable barrier to the reception of the gospel
by Mohammedans.

While I was at Luxor the Patriarch of the Copts
came there in a course of visitations to the several
Churches on the Upper Nile, and was received apparently with as much favour by the Moslems as by
the Christian population. The whole village turned
out to see him as he rode on a richly caparisoned
horse through the streets, and the English consul had
a reception in his honour, to which I had the privilege of an invitation. My conversation with him
could only be carried on through an interpreter, as
he knew no other language but Arabic, and I little

or nothing of this. He was very kindly and civil, and expressed a wish that I should visit him in his own house, on my return to Cairo. The little I saw of the Copts impressed me in their favour, and a young man who gave me some lessons in Arabic was a good specimen of the middle class—a Christian, I thought him, not only in name, but in deed and in truth.

The bazaars at Luxor are poor, but there is a good market once a week, which is crowded by the country people, who come in to dispose of their vegetables and fowls, which are displayed to the best advantage in a large open space on the borders of the town, where sellers and buyers congregate. Here, as elsewhere in the town, are the dancing-girls, clad in their gay dresses of pink, and yellow, and white, and blue. They are known as "ghawazee." One or two of them were pretty enough, but generally they are coarse-looking, and not unfrequently repulsive; and when we remember their character and profession, we must regard them with the greatest pity and compassion. I never saw them dance, but a gentleman on the steamer who witnessed the performance, said that the exhibition was indecorous to a degree, and that he was glad when it was over. These poor girls may be seen at the "bars," and in the "cafés," and take part in those wild orgies known as a "fantasía."

One other place we visited at Luxor was the English burying-ground. It is a dreary, arid, barren spot, surrounded by a mud wall, one tomb lying outside the enclosure. Among others, a brother of Sir Wilfrid Lawson's lies here, and the wife of Sir Valentine Baker. It was painful to see the sandy, neglected, ugly appearance of the little cemetery; great was the contrast it presented to an English village church-yard, with its spreading yews, and dark green cypresses, and well-tended smooth turf. I was glad to find that an effort was being made by the English visitors to put the place in order, and to make pro-vision for its being well kept in the future, and it was with more than satisfaction that I pleaded at one of the Sunday services in the hotel that the offertory should be devoted to this purpose. A considerable sum was the result. If the friends of those who lie in that repulsive cemetery knew of its condition, I believe they would gladly help to put it in order, and to give it an aspect more in accordance with that bright hope which the Christian has when he lays his dead in the grave.

KARNAK BY MOONLIGHT.

Come, stand with me in this great column'd hall,
And let the mellow moonlight clasp us round.
Make bare thy head ; is not this holy ground ?
Mark how each sculptur'd pylon, gate, and wall,
The granite obelisk, so fair and tall,
Which great Queen Hatasou raised on that mound,
Shine like to silver, while from bound to bound
All is lit up as though for festival.

Never did moon more luminously bright,
Make each carved lotus pillar gleam like snow,
Or set a crown of glory on the night,
For e'en the very shadows seem to glow—
Think you such glories flashed upon the sight
Of great Rameses centuries ago ?

CHAPTER XXIX.

Leave Luxor.—Arrival at Kenneh.—Visit to the Town.—
Belliâneh.—Ride to Abydos.—The Temples of Seti and
Rameses.—-The Kom-es-Sultán.—Ride back to Belliâneh.
—Religion of the Ancient Egyptians.

I T was with great regret that we left Luxor, about
the middle of February. The weather was
growing very hot ; but sunshine and warmth are
like life to me, and I would willingly have remained
some weeks longer. However, all things pleasant
must come to an end ; and so, having said farewell
to many friends, we got on board the *Mohammed
Ali*, a boat which from former experience we knew
well, and liked, and steamed down the Nile as far as
Kenneh.

We went on shore, and mounted, after the usual
struggle with the Arabs, the donkeys which were
waiting our arrival, some of them very fine animals,
and rode to the town, which is a large one, in order
to see the manufacture of porous water-jars and
earthen bottles, which are much used throughout

Egypt. On my way there I met what does not speak well for the civilization of this part of the country—a man walking along the road stark naked, and apparently without any idea of bashfulness. I had seen the same thing once before at Luxor ; and the man then showed no sense of shame, but strode along in the most unconcerned manner. At Kenneh there is quite a colony of dancing-girls, and we saw them in their gay and flimsy attire, flitting like butterflies through the shops and bazaars. After making some purchases of goollehs, which are wonderfully cheap, and of long polished sticks, which are prettily made, we returned to the boat, and remained at anchor that night.

The following morning we left for Belliâneh, a large town from which Abydos and its noble temple is visited. By the way, is the name of this village to be pronounced short or long? Is it, as I heard it generally called, Abȳdos, or is it, in accordance with the name of the Greek town, Abȳdos? Some pronounce it one way, and some the other. It is a ride of six miles from Belliâneh to Abydos, the ancient Thinis, or This, the oldest city of Egypt, from which Mena, the first king of the 1st dynasty,—whom Sir G. Wilkinson places 2,320 years before Christ, Mariette Bey 5,004, and Dr. Brugsch Bey 4,400,—

migrated to found Memphis. We started at once on
our ride, that we might not only escape the burning
heat of the day, but have as much time as possible
to spend amongst the ruins of a temple where Osiris
is said to be buried. We had a pleasant ride, past
several small hamlets, standing in groves of palm,
and with battlemented dovecotes, through large fields
of beans, now in pod, and of a strong growth, by
reason of the amazing fertility of the soil. There
were also fields of wheat and barley, all irrigated by
hundreds of little rills, through the labour of the
industrious Fellaheen. The bright green of the
luxuriant crops was refreshing to the eye, and a
grateful exchange from the blinding and burning
sands. Boys met us on the way with their slings,
made of the fibre of the palm, and showed us their
skill in sending stones high in the air and across the
tracts of corn. You purchase a sling as a matter of
course, though you know too well that you will not
be able to use it with the dexterity of these boys,
who, by their practised art, keep off the birds from
the precious grain.

We spent a long morning and afternoon in the
two grand temples of Abydos. These are the temple
of Seti and the temple of Rameses. The temple
of Seti I. was founded by this king, of the 19th

dynasty, the father of Rameses II. It is famous for the bas-relief on its walls. As Seti and Rameses are represented together in the sculptures, it is supposed that when the temple was built, they were reigning conjointly on the throne. The temple is dedicated to seven gods; has seven vaulted naves, leading into seven sanctuaries, which are severally consecrated to Osiris, Isis, Hathor, Phtah, Harmachus, and Horus, the king himself being pictured as one of the divinities. There are two magnificent halls of columns open to the sky. On the western wall is the tablet of Abydos, and here Seti and Rameses are represented, the one offering the sacrifice of fire, the other reciting the sacred hymn. Before them are the cartouches of seventy-six kings, beginning with Mena, or Menes, and ending with Seti himself; and these each offer libations to their ancestors. In a court, not far from this, is a fine sculpture of Seti and Rameses taming a splendid wild bull, evidently the work of a great artist. We learn the interesting fact from Mr. Stanley Lane Poole that the sculptor's name was Hi. He must have been a man of great genius and power of execution, as nothing could surpass the bas-relief, or intaglio relievato, of this bull. The intaglio relievato was a style of sculpture introduced by Rameses II. It was in this temple that the "Tablet of Abydos," containing a chronological table of kings, was discovered, and from this temple it was taken to the British Museum, where it may now be seen.

The Kom-es-Sultán is a mound formed by the accumulation, through many centuries, of tombs of Egyptians whose bodies were brought from all parts to be buried here close to Osiris, for it was believed that under Kom-es-Sultán the head of Osiris was interred. We have seen that Philæ contested with Abydos the honour of being the burial-place of Osiris; and it would seem that the old Egyptian oath, " By him who sleeps in Philæ," decided the question by general consent.

After some pleasant hours at Abydos, where we were much impressed with the beauty and interest of the temple, so perfect in many of its courts and sculptures, we rode back in the calm beauty of the evening through the fields of barley, and beans, and wheat, past the little villages, to Belliâneh, where the boat was moored.

The religion of the ancient Egyptians is a subject of great interest. Dr. Wallis Budge, who has given much study to the subject, and is recognised as an authority, states that the Egyptians acknowledged the unity, eternity, and infinity of the Deity, as well as His loving-kindness; and that when in their moral maxims they used the word " God," they referred to a being with the attributes just named. In proof of this he quotes the verses of an old hymn. And yet, notwithstanding this idea, we know "they had gods many, and lords many." Every nome, or district, had its own special triad, whom it delighted to honour, just as Brahma, Vishnu, and Sivah, the creator, preserver, regenerator, are worshipped by Hindus. The triad of Philæ was Osiris, his sister and wife Isis, and Horus his son. At Thebes the triad worshipped was Ammon-Ra, the great sun-god ; Maut, the universal mother ; and Chonsu. At Memphis, the triad held in honour were—Phtah, the Vulcan of the Egyptians, the creative principle and lord of truth ; Pasht, or Bast, always known by the cat's head; and Apis, the sacred bull, an incarnation of Osiris. At Heliopolis, the city of the sun, the triad consisted of the great god Ra, the son of Nu, or the sky, and the Mnevis bull, and Osiris. The sun-god Ra died every night, but created himself anew each morning. The Egyptians had several other gods in their pantheon : Thoth, the god of letters, represented with the head of an ibis, and sometimes crowned with the disc of the full moon ; Nephthys, the wife of Set, the demon who conquered Osiris; Hathor, supposed to be a form of Isis ; and Sekket and Bast, to whom the cat and the lion were sacred. Egyptologists differ widely as to the charac-

ter of the Egyptian religion, some believing that the
innumerable gods of the pantheon were but manifes-
tations of the attributes of the one eternal God.
Mariette Bey says that " we nowhere find in the
temples that unique, invisible Deity, without name
and without form, who was supposed to hover about
the highest summit of the Egyptian pantheon." From
a study of the temple of Denderah, he concludes that,
according to the Egyptians, " the universe was God
Himself, and that pantheism formed the foundation of
their religion." There can be no doubt that on whatever their religion was based, whether on the belief of
a spiritual God, or on pantheism, or on a solar myth,
it degenerated, and developed into a grossly material
faith. It may have been at first that some lofty minds
saw a great presiding spirit behind these many
material forms ; but the ignorant would lose the substance in the shadow, and simply pay their homage to
the birds and to the beasts which filled the sacred
shrines. In *Egypt's Place in History,*[1] Bunsen remarks
well : " In the animal worship of Egypt, the animals
were to be mere symbols, but became, by the inherent
curse of idolatry, real objects of worship." The number
of gods, bestial and human—the Pharaohs being deified

---

[1] Vol. iv. p. 640.

—seem to me to contradict the general belief of Egyptologists, that the Egyptians were monotheists, and
had a deeply seated belief in the supreme intelligence.
I agree with Mr. Andrew Lang in the view he has
stated in *Egyptian Divine Myths;* namely, that "the
bestial shapes in which the gods were clad had no
allegorical character ; they denote that straightfor-
ward worship of the lower animals which is found in
many religions, ancient and modern." But if it be the
case, as Maspero believes, that the religion of the
Egyptians, at first pure and spiritual, became grossly
material in its later developments, and that the old
faith degenerated, this is only in accordance with
human nature ; it is repeated in the history of Churches
calling themselves Christian. The picture or the
image becomes in process of time an object of worship, although the apology for placing it in the holy
place is that it is not intended as such, but is meant
to raise the thoughts in adoration to Him whom it
represents. Hence the danger of symbolism ; the
mind is arrested by the figure or painting, and stays
there, instead of ascending to the One Supreme Being
who is alone the object of adoration. How wise, then,
in God to forbid the Hebrews to " make any graven
image, or likeness of Himself, or, indeed, of anything that is in heaven above, or in the earth beneath,

or in the water under the earth." He knew what snares they might prove, and that the heart is naturally prone to a sensuous worship and idolatry. And whereas the Egyptians kept in the adytum of all their temples a sacred animal—hawk or crocodile, jackal or cat—just as the Greek and the Roman placed in their sanctuaries the statue of the god, the Hebrews were commanded to worship in a shrine without an idol, and no image was to have a place in the holy of holies of the Jewish temple.

CHAPTER XXX.

THE *Rameses* remained that evening at Belliâneh, and on the next morning, Friday, the
24th of February, left for Assiout, which we reached
about 3.30 in the afternoon. We landed at once, and
I took the opportunity of visiting the new and fine
Theological College and Boarding and Day Schools
of the American Mission, situated in a good and open
part of the town, and standing near a grove of the
date palm. They are in every way adapted to the
wants of this admirable institution, and are doing
good work. For nine years the school here was a free
day school, often struggling for life against the pre-
judice and superstitions of the people, and the fierce
opposition of the Coptic clergy ; but after years of
labour and disappointment, a suitable site was obtained in 1874, and a building erected. The Boarding

School has grown steadily in strength and influence, and is open to all who choose to attend—Moslems, Copts, Jews, Protestants, and Greek Catholics. The school is patronized by all classes, and is favourably recognised by the Government. The students are accorded the same exemption from service as is accorded to students in the great Moslem University El Azhar, at Cairo. Those who are able pay tuition fees; and numbers of all faiths are glad to avail themselves, not only of the secular instruction which is given, but also of the religious training, which is made a *sine quâ non* of attendance. Some tell us that it is impossible to convert a Moslem, but the total of those baptized in Assiout and in other quarters of the Mission is sixty; and one of the head clerks at present in the Assiout Post Office was a Mohammedan, baptized at Assiout while he was a student at the College. One Ahmed Fahney, son of a Government official at Cairo, was baptized in 1877, was withdrawn quietly from the country to save him from persecution or death, studied at Edinburgh, and is now a medical Christian missionary at Amoy, in China. To say that it is impossible to convert a Moslem is not only contradicted by facts, but is a direct impeachment of the power of God's Word, and of the grace of the Spirit, and brands with the imputation of folly our Saviour's command to "go into all the world, and preach the Gospel to every creature." The Mohammedan surely is not excluded from the glad tidings; he is to form no exception to the mercy of God. As the question of Mohammedanism has been much discussed lately, I was anxious to discover its effects on the people of the country, and so made many inquiries as to its influence from those who, being for many years residents in Egypt, had every opportunity of observation. Some of these being directly connected with missionary effort among the people, were able to speak with authority on the subject. In every instance the opinion was unfavourable; and from what I observed myself, I believe that it has failed in Egypt, as elsewhere, to civilize, or to elevate, or purify the people. As Sir William Muir says in his *Annals of the Early Caliphate:* "Polygamy and secret concubinage are still the privilege, or the curse of Islam, the worm at its root, the secret of its fall. By these the unity of the household is fatally broken, and the purity and virtue weakened of the family tie; the vigour of the dominant classes is sapped; the body politic becomes weak and languid excepting for intrigue; and the throne itself liable to fall a prey to doubtful or contested successors. . . . Hardly

less injurious is the power of divorce, which can be
exercised without the assignment of any reason whatever, at the mere word and will of the husband. It
not only hangs over each individual household like
the sword of Damocles, but affects the tone of society
at large ; for even if not put in force, it cannot fail as
a potential influence, existing everywhere, to weaken
the marriage bond, and detract from the dignity and
self-respect of the sex at large." The Cadi in Cairo
told a friend of mine, long a resident there, that he
was disgusted with his office, for he was engaged all
day in writing out papers of divorce for married men,
and in filling up other papers for their re-marriage.
Nor does this facility of divorce and re-marriage
prevent vice, and that of the worst description ; nor
does it free the country from professional outcasts ;
indeed, it is said that many of the poor women, often
mere girls, who are put away by their husbands, frequent that quarter of Cairo known as " The Women's
Bazaar." Islam cannot foster purity or chastity. If
the heaven of the Mohammedan consists largely in
the possession of a number of beautiful Houris, who
are to minister to the enjoyment of the faithful, surely
this gives a sanction to the idea that the indulgence
of the senses is the chief good. Why not, therefore,
make earth, as far as possible, a sensual Elysium, and

so conform it to the Paradise for which they look after death? I know of nothing that can be more degrading and defiling for man than a lifelong expectation of unbridled sensuality in the other world as their reward, or more crushing or hopeless for woman than the idea of annihilation after death ; and this, whatever Mohammed may have said, is, I believe, the popular creed of the Moslem people. Again, it is marvellous that any one can say that Islam is "not an anti-Christian faith, but a half-Christian faith,—an imperfect Christianity ;" for with a professed respect for Christ as a prophet, it denies His oneness with the Father, and with His equality with God, His atonement and mediation, and subordinates Him and His teachings to Mohammed and the Korán. And is not the Moslem faith so intolerant of Christianity that persecution and death are often the penalties that attend those who abandon Mohammed for Christ? Islam dooms the nations which have accepted it to a low and, in some respects, a barbarous condition. It is immovable. It is, as Mr. Palgrave says in his *Arabia*, vol. i. p. 372, "in its essence stationary, and was framed thus to remain. Sterile like its god, lifeless like its first principle and supreme original in all that constitutes true life,—for life is love, participation, and progress, and of these the Koranic Deity has none,—it justly

repudiates all change, all advance, all development."
Then, as regards its religion, does it not mainly consist
of that " bodily exercise " which "profiteth little " ?
The Moslem's prayer may be as mechanical an exercise as the turning of the prayer-wheel in Tibet, for
the words of the prescribed ritual need not be even
understood, and nothing more is required than that
the words be repeated in Arabic, and in the position
which is prescribed. All that is needed for a Mohammedan's salvation is to repeat these prayers five times
a day, to give alms, and observe the yearly fast of the
Ramazan, and make himself, or by deputy, the pilgrim-
age to Mecca,—let him do this, and Paradise and the
Houris are his for evermore. Islam has no great ideals
or high aspirations,—has nothing to attract the noblest
minds, or to constrain them to dare all things, and to
count all things but loss, if they can only reach the
lofty standard which is proposed to their hope. Christianity holds out an ideal of life in its humility, its
purity, its self-denial and toleration, its forgiveness of
injuries, and its brotherly love, altogether unknown
to the religion of Islam ; and, therefore, one rejoices
at every attempt such as those made by the American
Missions, and Miss Whately's admirable schools at
Cairo, to propagate Christianity, and to win men to
the knowledge and love of its Founder.

On our return from the colleges and bazaars of Assiout,—the latter good, and full of tempting things, some of which were irresistible,—we reached the steamer, and found another boat, the *Tewfik*, anchored close beside her for the night. We received a friendly invitation from the people on board the ship to spend the evening with them, offering the attractions of music ; and this the greater part of the passengers on our boat accepted with pleasure. They were going up the Nile, we were going down ; and we were mutually glad to meet, and to wish one another " good speed." The evening was a very agreeable one, and the music, both vocal and instrumental, was excellent.

The following morning, Saturday, February 25th, we left Assiout at an early hour, and had a beautiful day for our course northward. On Sunday we had Divine service as usual, and soon after the khamseen wind, hot as from a furnace, and carrying with it dusky clouds of fine sand, began to blow. The khamseen is a wind from the south, and is so called from its blowing at intervals during a period of fifty days. The days when the khamseen blows are most trying and exhausting ; the skin becomes parched and dry ; the breathing is quickened ; there is a dislike to any exertion, and the very life seems to go out of you. It was so all Sunday ; but in the evening the

T

wind sank, and the air grew cooler. About seven o'clock we ran upon a sandbank, and the boat was not set free until three o'clock the next morning. But the delay, and the stillness of the steamer while she lay wedged in the sand, gave us the opportunity of examining quietly the largest and most beautiful halo I ever saw round the moon. That "orbèd maiden, with white fire laden," was surrounded by a luminous milk-white circle, coloured with all rainbow tints, and bright with every prismatic hue. The planet herself, within two days of being at the full, was singularly brilliant, and the sky was clear and full of stars. The halo lasted for some time, then very gradually began to dissolve, then slowly melted away, and the moon walked on in her glory, and made the night seem but a paler day. It was pleasant that our last evening on the Nile should be marked by so lovely a phenomenon, for in very deed

> " A thing of beauty is a joy for ever ;
> Its loveliness increases, it will never
> Pass into nothingness, but still will keep
> A bower quiet for us, and a sleep
> Full of sweet dreams, and health, and quiet breathing."

CHAPTER XXXI.

Cairo.—Mosque of Ibrahim Agha.—The Khedivial Library.—
The Pyramids by Moonlight.—Coptic Churches.—Cele-
brating the Holy Communion.—A Coptic Wedding.—
Choosing a Wife.—An Egyptian Dinner.

A MONTH'S stay in Cairo gave us the opportunity
of seeing many things we had left unseen on
our former visit. We rode to the Mokattam hills,
where the prospect is much the same as that from
the Citadel, though more extensive, and commanding
a wider view of the Nile, the Pyramids, and the Desert
as far as Helouan. A mosque which will repay a
visit is that of Ibrahim Agha, which has an interesting court shaded with green palms ; but what is most
worth seeing there is the wall of the Leewan-el-Kibleh,
which is lined throughout with blue porcelain tiles,
wrought into the representation of some cypress trees,
and exhibiting very beautiful and artistic work. Those
who would like to see some fine specimens of mushre-
beeyeh work, and some good examples of brass

tables, and mosque lamps in brass and glass, also some carved ivory book-stands and inlaid doors, should pay a visit to the museum of Arabic antiquities which are to be seen in the old mosque of Hakim.

The Khedivial library should by no means be passed over; for here will be found the fine collection of illuminated copies of the Korán, brought here from the mosques where they had lain for centuries; and one of them, in the old Kufic characters, is said to be nearly 1,200 years old. The leaves of many of the copies are richly decorated with Arabesque scrolls, and the writing and the letters exhibit great beauty of form.

All who have the opportunity should see the Pyramids by moonlight. At the invitation of one of the officers in command at Cairo, we dined at the little hotel which is close to those giant sepulchres which have stood for thousands of years on the border of the Libyan desert. In the evening we walked, in the light of a moon just past the full, to the base of those stupendous monuments, as they rose in all their grandeur and majesty to the sky studded with many a star. The whole scene was impressive : the stillness,—for the Arabs who accompanied us were silent,—the vast Pyramids themselves, the earliest monuments of civilized man. But even more impressive was the great Sphinx, as it raised its colossal human head on high, over the desert sands. Its mutilated features were softened by the tender light, and it was possible to believe that it might have had the beauty and the grace, and the winning smile, described by Abd-el-Lalif with so graphic a pen. When we had sat for some time looking at "the Father of Terrors," we turned away with a crowd of solemn feelings as we thought of those who in the unknown past had sculptured this mysterious monument out of the natural limestone rock.

One of the most interesting of the churches in Cairo is an old Coptic church, Aboo Sirgeh, which has some fine woodwork carved with the figures of St. George, the patron saint of the Copts, and with familiar Scripture subjects. It contains a subterranean chapel, in the side aisle of which are two niches ; and there is a tradition that when the holy family fled into Egypt, the Virgin and the infant Jesus rested in one niche and Joseph in the other. El Abra is another Coptic church worthy of a visit, and it is known as " El Maalláka," or " the suspended," because it is situated high up in one of the towers of the Roman gateway of Babylon, and you have to reach it by a lofty staircase. This Roman gateway was given the name of " Babylon," because it was founded by people from that country, who were descendants of captives taken by Rameses II., and were permitted by the kings of Egypt to have their dwelling-place here.

While in Cairo, I attended a Coptic service in the cathedral in the Copt quarter. It is a large, handsome building, standing in a narrow street, which runs off from the Shariá-Waj-el-Birkit, opposite the Hotel Royal. The Coptic schools are close to the church. It has a large centre, and two side aisles, and a small apse towards the east. There is a screened gallery running round the building supported by pillars, which is intended for women. There are wooden seats on each side of the church, and a reading-desk, on which rests the Bible. I went in about nine o'clock, and the service had then been going on for two hours. The congregation of men was not large, but the court was filled with women and children, who probably had attended the first part of the service. The Patriarch was not present. The priest was ministering in the apse, robed in white vestments, and the lessons were read in Coptic by a layman, and translated into Arabic by a young man in a surplice. I heard that the lessons, the Gospel, and the Lord's Prayer, are the only parts of the service that are translated ; and as the Coptic is a dead language, the other portions of its liturgy cannot be understood by the common people, and must, therefore, necessarily be unprofitable. After this part of the service was over, I went into a small chapel behind the apse, and there found a priest in rich vestments of white satin engaged in celebrating the Holy Communion. He was ministering with some acolytes inside a circular chancel, into which there were several openings on three sides. A number of men were standing watching the consecration and the elevation of the elements, and were looking eagerly over one another's heads at the different parts of the ceremonial. None of these, however, partook of the sacred elements. The only communicants were children, boys and girls, and they received in both kinds, the bread being, so far as I could see, dipped in the wine and placed by the priest in their mouths. After receiving, the children held up their aprons to their faces, or put their handkerchiefs before their mouths, and waited within the screen until all had communicated, and the blessing was given from the altar. Then the priest, before taking off his vestments, sprinkled the people with holy water, gave the bread that remained over, through the screen, to the people, who pressed forward anxious to receive it from his hands ; and as I was standing near, he offered me a part of the cake which he had blessed, and which I took.

The Coptic Church has resisted all attempts at reform, and retains the same religious orders, and the same peculiar rites and customs, which it had in the beginning, when it was condemned by the Council of Chalcedon for holding the doctrines of the Euty-chians.

I had an opportunity of seeing a Coptic wedding, and being present at an Egyptian dinner. The invitation was received through the kindness of Dr. Lansing, the principal of the American Mission in Cairo. The bridegroom was a young Copt, and the bride the child of Coptic parents, but having been educated in the American Mission schools, had become a Protestant. So far as one could see through her veil, she was dark-eyed and pretty. Through a mistake in the hour I missed the actual marriage ceremony, but was present at the bridegroom's house when he led his bride home. There is great rejoicing on such occasions : processions through the streets on foot or in carriages, with bands of music, sometimes dancing, and all that can lend a joyousness to the auspicious event. When I, and the members of my party who were included in the invitation, went to the house at seven o'clock in the evening, we found the street leading to it illuminated with coloured lamps. The court in which the house stood, and the lower rooms, were crowded with friends and relatives of the happy pair, and brilliantly lighted up. There was also a band of music, with drums and hautboys, and a chorus of singers who sang in their own peculiar fashion, which is anything but harmonious to a Western ear. The singing of the Egyptians, whenever I had the opportunity of hearing it, consisted in a low, monotonous drawl, which was devoid of air or tune. After staying a short time in a room below, we were taken upstairs to the chamber where the bride was sitting, and where she was receiving the congratulations of her friends. In a neighbouring apartment were more hired female singers, who had various instruments in their hands, to the sound of which they were singing the happiness of lovers, and the praises of the bride, in imagery not very unlike that used in the "Song of Solomon." The bride was veiled; and though she had been betrothed seven days before, and was married in the afternoon of the day I speak of, yet she had never seen her husband, nor had he ever seen her, except as we saw her, through her veil. Nor was he to have the privilege of looking in her unveiled face for seven days more. It is the mother of the bridegroom who usually arranges

a marriage. She goes among her friends to find a
wife for her son ; and when, after much inquiry, she
discovers the girl whom she thinks in every way
suitable, she informs her son, who is influenced by
her opinion, and commits the arrangements to her
judgment. Sometimes the choice of the bride is
left to women whose profession it is to select a fitting
bride for the man who employs them, and to open the
preliminary negotiations. There is naturally a good
deal of risk in this; but as women are so entirely
secluded in the East—as they are shut out from their
legitimate place in society—such an arrangement
becomes necessary, and so husband and wife are
married without ever having looked into one another's
face. If a Mohammedan is not pleased with the wife
chosen for him, he can send her off the next day, and
divorce her on the slightest pretext. And no doubt
his ignorance of the woman that he marries is a
stimulus to divorce. The Coptic religion does not
permit of divorce; and so the husband and wife,
who are wedded, literally, without knowing anything
of each other but what they learn through hearsay,
are one until death.

There was a long interval between our arrival at the
house and the dinner which followed. It was rather
a weary time, too ; for after our congratulations to the

bride, who understood and spoke English, and who looked very shy and timid, and must have been nearly worn out by the long ceremonies of the day, we had nothing to do but to talk to one another, or attempt a little conversation with the bridegroom and his friends, or sit still and listen to the monotonous music. At last came the dinner. A party of ten sat down on low chairs round a large brass tray ; and on this the various dishes were served, one at a time. We began with a bowl of soup, into which each dipped his spoon ; and this was followed by no less than sixteen courses, consisting of various kinds of meat, kebóbs of mutton, a pilaff of rice, vegetables, a roast turkey, and various kinds of jellies and cream. Our hands and fingers served us instead of knives and forks, and we pulled off as delicately as we could fragments of the turkey,—now a wing, now a piece of the breast,—or tore off a morsel of lamb, and transferred it to our plates, and so to our mouths. When the sweets were put on the table, we were given spoons, without which it would have been impossible to eat the pudding or the creams. The drinks were water, and lemonade, and a red-coloured wine ; but we preferred the cooler beverages. It was a dinner under difficulties, and though novel, not altogether agreeable. Though the dishes were well cooked, and quickly

served, we were not sorry when it was over, and
water was given us in brass basins, and Turkish
towels were placed at our service, that we might wash
and dry our hands. When this was done, we returned
to the bride's chamber, and after a short time there
we rose to say " Good-night," and to wish her and her
husband much happiness in the days to come. The
bridegroom's brother, a handsome man, offered us
pipes and coffee, and entreated us to stay longer,
and hear the band, composed of violins and tambou-
rines, and to listen again to the chorus of singing-
women. But we had had something too much of
this, and besides, it was getting late—past eleven
o'clock—so we begged to be excused. As we passed
through the lower rooms and the outer court, they
were thronged as upon our arrival ; and it seemed very
evident that the festivities were only at their height,
and would be prolonged far into the morning. On
leaving the house, we found the streets crowded with
carriages and people, and the coloured lamps were
still burning before the door.

CHAPTER XXXII.

The Island of Rodah.—The Nilometer.—Rise of the Nile.—
Cutting the Dam of the Canal El Khalig.—A Barbarous
Custom.—Effect of the Overflow.—An Imposing Spectacle
—Collection of Antiques.—Miss Whately's Schools.—
Popularity of the English in Egypt.

ON the island of Rodah, which is separated from
Cairo by the canal El Khalig, an Arab legend
places the site where the infant Moses was found by
Pharaoh's daughter as she went with her maidens to
wash herself in the river ; and there is a tall palm-
tree with a small white trunk which is called " Moses'
tree." The Nilometer, or well for measuring the
height of the inundation, is situate in a garden at the
southern extremity of the island. The Nile, which
has been gradually decreasing for nearly nine months,
begins to rise ; and its slow and steady progress is
watched with eager anxiety by the people. The
river reaches its greatest height towards the end of
September ; and every day during the inundation the

rise, as measured by the Nilometer, is proclaimed in
the streets of Cairo by public criers, and to each of
these is allotted a particular district.   An old law
enacts that no land tax can be levied until the river
has risen to the height of sixteen cubits in the Nilometer ; and the Government is accused of publish-
ing continually a false measurement, and thus it
compels the peasants to pay the tax upon their
farms before the due time.   If this be so, the Egyptian Government is as corrupt and oppressive as the
Turkish.   Perhaps the influence of the English occupation of the country may be able to correct this
abuse, as it has been the means of correcting others.
The inundation must be a wonderful sight :   the
gradual increase of the tranquil river ;   the growing
turbidness of the stream ;   its steady growth in volume,
until it assumes the appearance of a gigantic flood,
which covers the whole valley ;   when the Delta is
turned into a vast lake, and towns and villages are
like islands in the tumultuous waters, which rise to the
top of the natural banks, and flow along the base of
the artificial dykes by which the natural banks are
crossed.   Well might Jeremiah compare the invasion
of a mighty army to the inundation of this river :
" Who is this that cometh up as a flood, whose
waters are moved as the rivers?   Egypt riseth up

like a flood, and his waters are moved like the rivers : and he saith, I will go up, and will cover the earth ; I will destroy the city and the inhabitants thereof " (Jer. xlvi. 7, 8). The prophet Amos speaks of the desolation of a country under the same figure : " And the Lord God of hosts is He that toucheth the land, and it shall melt, and all that dwell therein shall mourn : and it shall rise up wholly like a flood ; and shall be drowned, as by the flood of Egypt " (Amos ix. 5).

As soon the Government issues a proclamation of " Full Nile," then ensues the ceremony of cutting the dam of the canal El Khalig. " The dam," as we read in Lane's *Modern Egyptians*, " is constructed before, or soon after the commencement of, the Nile's increase. The Khalig, or canal, at the distance of about 400 feet within its entrance, is crossed by an old stone bridge of one arch. About sixty feet in front of this bridge is the dam, which is of earth, very broad at the bottom, and diminishing in breadth towards the top, which is flat, and about three yards broad. The top of the dam rises to a height of about twenty-two or twenty-three feet above the level of the Nile when at the lowest, but not so high above the bed of the canal, for this is several feet above the low-water mark

of the river, and consequently dry for some months
when the water is low. The banks of the canal
are a few feet higher than the top of the dam.
Nearly the same distance in front of the dam that
the latter is distant from the bridge is raised a
round pillar of earth, diminishing towards the top
in the form of a truncated cone, not quite so high
as the dam. This is called the arûseh, or 'bride.'
Upon its flat top and on that of the dam, a little
maize or millet is commonly sown. The 'arûseh'
is always washed down by the rising tide before
the river has attained to its summit, and generally
more than a week or a fortnight before the dam
is cut.

"It is believed that the custom of forming this
arûsch arose from a superstitious usage, which is
mentioned by Arab authors, and among them by El
Makrize. This historian relates that in the year of
the conquest of Egypt by the Arabs, Amr-Ibn-El-As,
the Arab general, was told that the Egyptians were
accustomed, at the period when the Nile began to
rise, to deck a young virgin in gay apparel, and throw
her into the river, as a sacrifice to ensure a plentiful
inundation. This barbarous custom, it is said, he
abolished, and the Nile in consequence did not rise
in the least degree during a space of nearly three

months after the usual period of the commencement
of its increase. The people were greatly alarmed,
thinking that a famine would certainly ensue. Amr
therefore wrote to the Khalif to inform him of what
he had done, and of the calamity with which Egypt
was in consequence threatened. Omar returned a
brief answer, expressing his approbation of Amr's
conduct, and desiring him, upon the receipt of the
letter, to throw a note which it enclosed into the Nile.
The purport of this note was as follows :—'From
Abd Allah Omár, Prince of the Faithful, to the Nile
of Egypt. If thou flowest of thine own accord, flow
not; but if it be God, the One, the Mighty, who
causeth thee to flow, we implore God, the One, the
Mighty, to make thee flow!' Amr did as he was
commanded, and the Nile, we are told, rose sixteen
cubits in the following night."

No wonder there is great rejoicing when, at the
annual inundation, the river rises to its proper height;
for a full tide means plenty, and a low tide means
starvation. When the Nile retires, and leaves behind
its rich deposit of fertilizing mud, then all is ready
for the Fellaheen. No ploughing or harrowing is
needed ; they have only to "cast their bread"—their
seed-corn—"upon the waters," and afterwards to
bury it by means of toothless rakes, or palm-branches

U

wielded by men and boys, and then to wait for the rich and abundant harvest.

An event of some interest happened when I was in Cairo. This was the transference of the relics of Mohammed, collected at his death, and which had been placed in the office of the Administration of the Wakfs, to the mosque of Saïdna-el-Hussein. These relics consisted of the Prophet's shirt, a few hairs of his beard, his tooth-brush, and several other things. I had a good view of the streets from the Abdeen barracks, where one of the officers had kindly offered us a window from which to see the spectacle. The square of the Abdeen palace, which was close, was filled with 20,000 people ; and the whole of the route through which the procession was to pass was thronged, and presented a gay and brilliant appearance, as each of the religious corporations of the Mussulmans carried its own particular flag. The different dresses of the people who formed the crowd were wonderfully picturesque ; and the eye was charmed by the variety of colour. There were not only Egyptians, but Persians and Hindoos, and all who professed the faith of Islám. Each religious corporation had its own band of music, and each its own banner. There were 1,245 banners for seventy-five corporations. A salvo of guns from the Citadel announced the beginning of the ceremony. Four guards of horse police kept order in the streets. There was also a battalion of Egyptian infantry, preceded by music. More than 2,000 natives of position, Ulémas and sheykhs of the mosques ; fifty men carrying perfumes, and habited in rich costumes, preceded the grand Sheykh-el-Bakri, who bore the sacred relics, which were covered over with green satin, the colour of the Prophet. The Khedive appeared at the door of the Abdeen palace, but did not take part in the procession. But his chief officers were present — Sabet Pasha, chief of the cabinet, and Moukhtar Pasha, High Commissioner, and the ministers and high functionaries of state. It was an imposing and brilliant spectacle, and one well worth seeing ; and though there was an immense crowd of all nations and languages in the streets, the most perfect order was preserved, and there was no accident to record. In connection with one of these relics—Mohammed's tooth-brush—I may mention that the Prophet was very particular in enforcing the use of this, and wished it to be made of a certain kind of fibre, and that the teeth should be brushed horizontally. Before prayer he said the teeth were to be brushed, so that the mouth might be clean in addressing God. He laid down some stringent rules about this, all good in their way, but it is well to remember that the heart must be clean as well as the mouth ; for "out of the abundance of the heart the mouth speaketh,"—" out of this are the issues of life."

The best private collection of antiques in Cairo is that belonging to Dr. Grant, who for many years has been gathering together objects of great value, and has arranged them in historical order.   He has votive statuettes, mummy-cloths, jewellery, and a very large collection of royal scarabs, many of them dating back to early dynasties, and some of the greatest interest and beauty.   He has made Egyptology a study ; and his explanation of his really remarkable collection is a source of true enjoyment to all who take pleasure in Egyptian literature or art.   Amongst other valuable jewels he has the signet ring of Menephtah, the Pharaoh of the Exodus, which is cut and set with an artistic skill and taste not to be surpassed by the jewellers of the present day.   Dr. Grant most kindly opens his house on Wednesday evenings to friends and to strangers having an introduction to him ; and his enthusiasm for all that concerns the old Egyptians is so great, that he is never tired explaining the different objects in his rooms,—and a whole suite of chambers is filled with curiosities,—or giving you all the information he possesses   I spent several evenings at his house, and always found there a large and interested audience.[1]

It would be impossible, when speaking of Cairo, not to say a word or two about Miss Whately's schools. This estimable lady has devoted her time and her substance for twenty-six years to promote the temporal and spiritual good of the people of the city. At the request of Dean Butcher, the deservedly respected and popular chaplain of the English Church, to whose kindness and courtesy during my stay in Cairo I was much indebted, I had the privilege of pleading the cause of these schools before a large congregation. The schools contain 600 children— Moslems, Copts, Jews, and other races ; and the instruction includes, not only such secular knowledge as is given in the Government schools, and which will ensure the Government grant, but also directly Scriptural instruction out of that Word which God has " magnified above all His name." There is a medical mission connected with these schools, which affords

---

[1] While these sheets were passing through the press, I learnt with great regret that an attempt was made to rob Dr. Grant's house, and that he has lost many objects in his unrivalled collection. The robber, to distract attention, set fire to the house ; but fortunately the flames were extinguished before much damage was done. There is but one feeling for Dr. Grant— that of deep sympathy.

relief to a number of sufferers too poor to pay for
remedies ; and the patients, while waiting for advice,
have the beautiful and pathetic story of Jesus of
Nazareth read to them, and listen eagerly to what
they call " the good words."   The medical missionary
makes a yearly trip a little way up the Nile with
Miss Whately ; and in the course of a short excursion, no less than 300 patients have had their ailments
attended to, many of the men gathering round the
doctor to hear of the Great Healer, and many of the
women sitting at Miss Whately's feet as she reads of
the Syro-Phœnician woman who came to the Son of
man with a cry upon her lips for her daughter, and
of that other woman who, with a timid hand, laid
hold of the fringes of His robe, believing there was
healing in the touch.   Many who were able to read,
begged books for themselves, or for their sons, who
attended the village schools.   It is an interesting fact
about the young men trained in these schools, and
filling offices under Government, in the telegraph
offices, or in other departments, that not one during
the Egyptian war proved disloyal; all remained faithful to law and order.   I had on one occasion the
pleasure of addressing 150 young men, half of them
Mohammedans and half of them Copts, in Miss
Whately's large schoolroom, all of whom understood

English, and all of whom spoke English, and a most attentive audience I had. Such a free-will attendance of young men to hear an address founded on Holy Scripture, proves, I think, that there is a spirit of inquiry abroad, and that "the fields are white already unto harvest." The fact of English being taught in many of the schools, not only in the Delta, but in Upper Egypt, holds out the possibility that there may be soon in Egypt an English-speaking population ; and what an opening for mission work among the people this would be, and what a means, in the providence of God, of furthering the gospel ! Surely all that remains for those who believe that Christianity is immeasurably superior to Mohammedanism, who accept the truth that there is none other name whereby we can be saved but Christ's, is to obey the marching orders of the Great Captain of our salvation, and "preach the gospel " to those who hold the false faith of Islám. The French are wise in their generation; and I understand that their Government subsidizes those schools in which the French language is taught, and by these means endeavours to gain an influence in Egypt, and a hold over the population. Why should not England give some pecuniary assistance to the schools where English is made a part of the curriculum, and so maintain and extend the hold

she has got on the people through the occupation of
the country ?   From all that I could learn, the English
are popular, and the army popular with the Egyptians, except, perhaps, with those who from interested
motives dislike a righteous rule ; for the natives
believe that the English will, as far as possible, save
them from oppression, and see that justice is done ;
and they know, and rejoice to know, that the system
of the corvé, or forced labour, is being gradually done
away, and they entertain the hope that it will soon
cease altogether.

CHAPTER XXXIII.

Remarks on the Situation of the Land of Goshen.—Lake Mœris.
—Mr. Cope Whitehouse's Scheme.—Visit to Bubastis.
Excavations.—Ruins of the Temple.—Statues and Sculp-
tures.—M. Naville's Description of the Discovery of a
Remarkable Statue.—Other Valuable Discoveries.

I HAD the pleasure of making the acquaintance
of Mr. Cope Whitehouse, and of having many
interesting conversations with him on his theory of
the situation of the land of Goshen, a matter which is
still disputed. He places the land of Goshen, where
the Israelites found perennial pasturage, in the
Fayoum, "between Upper and Lower Egypt, from
On, which is Heliopolis, past Rameses-Memphis, for
fifty miles or more to the southward, and thus westward into the region of Mœris." To prove his point,
he has published a pamphlet with maps, called "The
Bahr Yusuf and the Prophecy of Jacob," which is full
of interest, and very ingenious—a pamphlet which cannot be read without profit and pleasure, whether his

conclusions be accepted or not. His arguments are not to be put aside hastily and without thought. Mr. Cope Whitehouse, who is full of enthusiasm, is widely known from a scheme which he has submitted to the Egyptian Government for forming a reservoir in the Fayoum, which, at high Nile, shall store the superabundance of the water, and allow it to be utilized for irrigation when the river is low. I was present at a lecture he gave on the subject, in which he detailed his plan, and explained its feasibility. Herodotus mentions the existence of Lake Mœris, and says : "It is yet more astonishing than the labyrinth which is close by." " The water in this lake does not spring from the soil, for these parts are excessively dry ; but it is conveyed through a channel from the Nile, and for six months it flows into the lake, and six months out again into the Nile." And Strabo, some 400 years later, speaking of Lake Mœris, says: " The Lake Mœris, by its magnitude and depth, is able to sustain the superabundance of water, which flows into it at the time of the rise of the river, without overflowing the inhabited and cultivated parts of the country. On the decrease of the water of the river, it distributes the excess by the same canal at each of the mouths ; and both the lake and the canal preserve a remainder, which is used for irrigation." Mr. Cope Whitehouse states that he has discovered at Wady Raian, some seventy miles to the south-west of Cairo, a basin of sufficient magnitude and depth to be converted into a great reservoir to store the superabundance of water at the annual inundation of the Nile. In the Wady Raian he believes he has discovered the Lake Mœris. It is admitted by Sir Colin Scott Moncrieff, who has investigated the subject, and has presented a report to the Council of Ministers, that "the realization of this scheme will be a very distinct benefit to Egypt;" but Sir Edgar Vincent, the financial adviser to the Egyptian Government, sees difficulties in the way, and entertains a doubt of the possibility of raising the necessary capital for a work of such labour and such cost. Whether the enthusiasm and courage of Mr. Cope Whitehouse will eventually be rewarded, and all obstacles be overcome, remains to be seen ; in the meantime he must be gratified that his project is lifted out of the realm of a visionary dream, and brought within the region of possible realization.

Before leaving Cairo, I paid a visit to Bubastis, in order to see the excavations which are being carried on there under the superintendence of M. Naville. ·Bubastis is about a quarter of a mile distant from Zagazig station, on the eastern side of the Delta. It lies between Memphis and Zoan, the capital of the

Hyksos, or Shepherd kings. About these Shepherd kings there is a good deal of mystery. In the words of Mr. Reginald Stuart Poole : " When they invaded the country, how they conquered it, how they ruled it, we do not know. All we can say is, that toward the close of their dominion they raised the monuments we see at Zoan, the great works of Apepi, who reigned about seventeen centuries before our era, and seems to have been the Pharaoh of Joseph. Here that patriarch became the regent of the Hyksos Pharaoh ; here Jacob came laden with years, and bowed with sorrow, to live near his favourite son ; and here the Hebrews came to make a home, to sow their seed, and thresh their harvests, and prosper in the land. When the Hyksos dynasty came to an end, and they were driven from the country, then a king of another dynasty arose 'who knew not Joseph ;' then began the Hebrew servitude, and 'their lives were made bitter with hard bondage, in mortar, and in brick, and in all manner of service in the field.' "

Bubastis is the Pi-beseth of the Bible; and here the goddess Bast, represented with the head of a lioness or a cat, was worshipped, and had her temple. Here reigned Shishak, the first king of the 22nd dynasty, who made an alliance with Jeroboam, and whose victory over the Jews in Palestine is recorded in the sculptures on the southern wall of the grand temple of Ammon-Ra, at Karnak.

To have as much time as possible at the ruins of Bubastis, and the day being very hot, we took a small carriage from the station at Zagazig to the site of the ancient city, and found there my friend the Rev. William Macgregor, who is connected with the Egypt Exploration Fund, and who introduced us to M. Naville, who is superintending the excavations. We walked over the cemetery of the Sacred Cats, strewn with the bones of these animals, and which was close to the tents of the officers of the Exploration Fund, and onward over the vast mounds which mark the perished city. The scene was a busy one. Hundreds of labourers were at work in a large pit—the excavated temple area—some clearing away the soil, some carrying it off in baskets, some digging in the trenches, while girls had bowls of water and sponges, carefully to wash the surfaces of carved pillars or statues, that all might be in readiness for the taking paper "squeezes." Mr. Macgregor told me that he had been anxious to photograph some of the women and girls who were employed in the work, but that they were so alarmed when they saw his camera, that they ran away in terror, with cries of affright, and could not be induced to stand for their portraits. They dreaded the evil eye, or some other fatal calamity. However, one or two were at last persuaded to do as he wished; and when the others saw the likenesses of their companions, they were so eager to be photographed, that now the difficulty was to resist their importunity to be taken. They were like children in their delight at seeing their own portraits.

The area of the temple was nearly cleared from end to end when I saw it; and M. Naville, whose courtesy is unfailing, pointed out the site of the great hypostyle hall, with its prostrate columns of the 12th dynasty workmanship, and a hall without columns, but containing bas-relief and sculptures, and numbers of finely executed hieroglyphic inscriptions. The columns of the hypostyle hall bear the cartouches of Rameses II.; and the columns of the festival hall are engraved with the names and titles of Osorkon II. of the 22nd dynasty, who reigned some 460 years later. The name of his queen, Karoama, is also engraven here. Various stones bear the name of Usertesen III.; and one is inscribed with the cartouche and titles of Pepi Merira, one of the Pyramid kings of the 6th dynasty, and the founder of the earliest temple of Denderah. M. Naville pointed out a beautiful Hathor head, and several mutilated statues of Rameses II., who here, as elsewhere, seemed to delight in the multiplication of his own image, and in representing himself in colossal magnitude. Two heads of this king have been found here,—one in black granite, with the crown of Upper Egypt, and one in red granite, wearing the helmet of Osiris. There are two statues of great interest to which our attention was directed by M. Naville. They are in black granite, and one is, unfortunately, headless ; the features of the other are damaged, but it is evident that the face is of the Hyksos type, and the head-dress, the " nems," with the uræus, is that of an Egyptian king. These statues prove that the Shepherd kings ruled in Bubastis. We also saw two fine statues of a scribe ; but, unhappily, the heads have been broken off. The black granite is finely polished, shines like a mirror, and is of beautiful substance. The figures sit with their legs crossed, and each holds on his lap a papyrus scroll, which is half unrolled, and on which are engraven his titles and his name. Each wears a loose dress fastened by braces, which are connected by an ornament not unlike a brooch ; and on this, and on his right shoulder, is cut the cartouche of Amenhotep III. Khuen-aten, or Amenhotep IV., has also left traces of his reign here in a sculpture representing the sacred oval of Aten-Ra, the disc-god. Khuen-aten, under the influence of his mother, who was a foreigner, changed the religion of Egypt, and introduced the worship of Aten-Ra, the sun's disc, for the Ammon-Ra of Thebes. He removed the seat or government from Thebes to Khooaten, which he founded, and which has been identified with the modern Tel-el-Amarna.

Very many other interesting objects have been discovered in these great ruins by M. Naville and his assistants, and the work of excavating must be to them a labour of love. If, as I understand, it is his opinion that the original temple was founded by Pepi I. of the 6th dynasty, who, according to Dr. Brugsch, lived about 3,300 years B.C., and if Nectanebo I. added to the vast pile, then the history of this temple has extended over a period of more than 3,200 years. One of the most remarkable of the statues is another of the Hyksos type, broken off at the waist, of which I will give M. Naville's description in his own words. It appeared in the *Times* of April 6, 1888.

"Our most important discovery up to the present time was made yesterday morning. I had noticed on Friday the corner of a block of polished black granite which I thought might belong to some good monument, and I had it unearthed yesterday. It proved to be the lower half of a life-size figure of very beautiful workmanship, with two columns of finely cut hieroglyphics, engraved down each side of the front of the throne to right and left of the legs of the statue. These inscriptions give the name and titles of an absolutely unknown king, who, judging from the work, must belong to the Hyksos period, or, at all events, to one of the obscure dynasties preceding the Hyksos invasion. I forward a copy of the inscriptions. One cartouche contains a sign which is quite new to me, and which I therefore cannot decipher. The other reads 'Ian-Ra,' or 'Ra-ian'—a name unlike any I have ever seen. He is described, most strangely, as the worshipper of his Ka (*i.e.*, his ghost, or double).

". . . Since writing the above, I have been over to Boulák, and have shown my copy of the inscriptions to Ahmed-Kemal-ed-Deen Effendi, the Mohammedan official attached to the museum. He was deeply interested, and said at once, 'That is the Pharaoh of Joseph. All our Arab books call him Reiyán, the son of El Welíd.' He then wrote the name for me in Arabic, which I enclose herewith. For my own part I know nothing of Arab literature or Arab tradition. I should not, however, be disposed to attach much weight to this curious coincidence. Still it *is* curious, and certainly interesting."

It may be well not to be too hasty in concluding that the statue with the cartouche, on which is the name Ian-Ra, is Joseph's Pharaoh, but it is possible that it is ; and Mr. F. D. Griffith, student attached to the Egypt Exploration Fund, in a letter to the *Times* of May 19, 1888, furnishes some additional evidence bearing on this possibility. He says, "The only Hyksos (shepherd) monument in the British Museum is a small lion in the northern vestibule. This monument is of Hyksos style, and bears a name that hitherto has baffled students. It is very indistinctly engraved. On examining it I feel convinced that the name is the singularly written throne name of Raian, as inscribed on the seat of the statue discovered by M. Naville. The date thus obtained is in harmony with the general opinion that Joseph ruled Egypt under one or more of the Hyksos Pharaohs."

Such are some of the valuable discoveries made by M. Naville and the officers of the Egypt Exploration Fund ; and all that is wanting to bring more wonders to light are funds to carry on the work. All who love the Bible, whose truth is illustrated by every new discovery, should, so far as they are able, help a fund which has done so much already to throw light upon the sojourn of the Israelites in the land of the Pharaohs. The discoveries made have been of the greatest interest to all who believe in the truth and accuracy of the Old Testament Scriptures, and have

confirmed the historical value of the Word of God.
M. Naville, in excavating on the banks of the Fresh-
water Canal, near Tel-el-Mashkûtah, has laid bare the
very store chambers which the Israelites built three
thousand three hundred years ago. The city thus
unburied is Pithom, the Succoth of the Hebrews, the
place where the Israelites halted on the first day of
their march out of Egypt. So that we have now
some guide to the route of the Exodus. Again, how
full of interest the discoveries of Mr. Flinders Petrie!
He it was who, in excavations carried on in the North-
eastern Delta, found the ruins of the palace of
Psammetichus I., described in the forty-third chapter
of Jeremiah as " Pharaoh's house at Tahpanhes," and
which was assigned by Pharaoh Hophra, son of
Psammetichus II., to the fugitive daughters of King
Zedekiah. Mr. Petrie discovered the very pavement
at the entry to the palace, when Jeremiah foretold
the conquest of Egypt by Nebuchadrezzar, king of
Babylon. What matchless treasures Mr. Petrie has
discovered lately in the Fayoum! He has discovered
the labyrinth described by Herodotus, and by means
of a fragment of hieroglyphed limestone has identified
the pyramidal tomb of its builder, Amenemhat III.,
of the 12th dynasty. He has discovered an extensive
cemetery of the Græco-Roman period, and has dis-

interred hundreds of mummies, and countless objects
of interest buried with the dead. He has also brought
to light a fine series of veritable portraits painted
on panels with a wax medium. Looking at these
portraits, you see the faces of men and women who
have been entombed for nearly two thousand years.
All who take an interest in art, archæology, and
history, should do what they can to rescue the priceless monuments of past ages from the graves in which
they lie entombed. Wealth could hardly be better
spent than in aiding to carry on researches in a
country so closely associated with sacred history, and
whose stupendous monuments " still present," as the
learned physician, Abd-el-Latif of Bagdad, says,
when describing Memphis, " a crowd of wonders that
bewilder the intellect, and which the most eloquent of
men would vainly attempt to describe."

CHAPTER XXXIV.

WE learn much of what the Bible calls "the wisdom of the Egyptians," from their monuments and temples and tombs. Some of the earliest records of our race are to be found written there— written, not in perishable materials, but graven on the hard rock. Had they been written with a pen on the papyrus, they might never have reached us, or come down uninjured through many thousands of years. What they wished to perpetuate, these old Egyptians sculptured on the chambers of their temples, or inscribed on the walls of their tombs. They fulfilled the aspiration of Job : "Oh that my words were now . . . graven with an iron pen and lead in the rock for ever!" The kings wished to perpetuate their memory

and their heroic deeds, and so they had hewn from
the granite quarry the colossal stones with which
they built their monuments, raised their obelisks, or
wrought their statues. On these they depicted, cut
into the stone, not only their principal deeds, but also
the minutest details of their daily life. The materials
with which they built, the climate, the pure atmosphere, the dry air of the desert, conspired to give
durability to the records, and ensure them against the
destroying hand of time. We know, therefore, the
domestic life of the old Egyptian. We see him in
his various pursuits—hunting, fishing, shooting, boat-
ing. We see him in his family: his wife sits by his
side, his children are close by, and his servants wait
upon his will. We learn how he amused himself:
musicians play on various instruments, others sing,
and others beat time with their hands, and women
dance before him for his pleasure. We know, too, his
thoughts about death and the life beyond the grave;
for in their tombs—palaces of the dead—hewn out
of the rock, with long galleries and halls—there are
sculptures of the barges which carry the mummy over
the sacred lake which was made near every chief city,
and pictures of the mysterious world where dwell the
gods of genii, good and evil. We see the goddess of
justice, with her single ostrich feather, and the forty-

two judges, and the balances of judgment, the heart being placed in one scale, and the symbols of truth and justice in the other. We learn, moreover, from their monuments, what advances they had made in art ; how they were well acquainted in architecture with the principle and use of the arch, centuries before it was introduced into Greece. That they had a fine perception of the beautiful we know from the forms of their columns, the graceful capitals of their pillars, often moulded after the shape of the lotus flower or papyrus plant, and also from the delicate workman-ship which they display. "The learning and wisdom of the Egyptians" had become a proverb in the days of Moses. Paintings brilliant in colour, though con-ventional in form, and marked by the angularity which is seen in the early pictures of the Italian and other schools, adorned their palaces. Amongst their other accomplishments, poetry was not forgotten. The poem of Pentaur, a poet in the days of Rameses II., was written on the southern wall of Karnak, and remains there to the present day, and has been trans-lated into English. They had, too, their hymns, full of noble sentiment, composed in honour of their gods. They made great advances in science, and were familiar with astronomy, as is shown by the paintings of the signs of the zodiac on some of their temple roofs. Herodotus tells us that in his days they were skilled in the art of medicine. "Each physician," he says, "applies himself to one disease only, and not more." There were in those early days, as now, oculists and dentists, specialists for ailments of the head, diseases of the heart, and internal disorders. One of the Biblical names of Egypt, "Ham," or Khem, is said to survive in the word "alchemy," chemistry being derived from the medical fame of ancient Egypt.

In very early ages, when other nations had hardly emerged from barbarism, the Egyptians were skilled in the working of metals and the cutting of gems. Not only did they know the use of iron, and copper, and tin, but they fashioned the gold and silver into most beautiful ornaments, and understood the setting of precious stones. I have seen gems, and beads, and scarabs wrought in jasper, cornelian, agate, onyx, garnet, emerald, and turquoise. The working of these stones displays great skill. The discovery of glass is generally ascribed to some Phœnician sailors, who, having lighted a fire of dried seaweed on the seashore, found the sand and alkali fused into a vitreous substance; but centuries before this the Egyptians must have used glass, for in the paintings of Beni-Hassan, executed in the reign of Osirtasen, upwards of 3,000 years ago, are to be seen figures of glass-blowers at their work.

And when we think on the wonders of this land of Egypt,—of the pyramid builders,—of the temples, magnificent even in ruins,—of the tombs, cut and sculptured in the wild cliffs, with their long halls and decorated galleries,—we must confess that there were giants in the earth in those days—giants in art and philosophy, in science and engineering. There is no doubt that the Israelites were employed in some of those colossal works which still speak of the sacrifice and toil of those by whom they were erected, and that they made bricks for the treasure-cities, and for the outer walls of many a magnificent city and temple and tomb.

But turn from these thoughts to one important truth, which, in my judgment, is to be learnt from the advance in art and science of the early Egyptians, and from the magnificence of their monuments and shrines. We must remember that we are dealing with facts that carry us back some thousands of years in the history of the world—to only a single generation after the Deluge. And it appears to me that we have in the early historic grandeur of Egypt a strong witness against the theory of evolution of man, as taught by Haeckel and others of his school, and held by their disciples. We are called upon by this theory to believe that man has been evolved out of the *monera*, —to hold that "there is no doubt that he is descended from an extinct mammalian form, which, if we could see it, we should certainly class with the apes ; and it is equally certain, we are assured, that this primitive ape in turn descended from an unknown semi-ape, and the latter from an extinct pouched animal." And this animal in its turn descended from another unlike creature ; and so on by successive steps backward, until the first shapeless, structureless mass of protoplasm is reached, which was, we are told, the true ancestor of man.

"Monera," as probably the reader knows, is the plural of the word "monern ; " and a monern is each individual living particle of this first structureless mass of protoplasm. But this does not account for the origin of life ; and therefore Haëckel assumes that at some time in the unknown past, life was introduced on our globe by spontaneous generation. This, however, is but the offspring of a scientific imagination, and is unsupported by proof. The assumption is introduced in order to get rid of the miraculous ; yet what could be more miraculous than such spontaneous generation. For life cannot be the product of inert matter, or of molecular motion, which the particles of matter themselves assume. Life can only be imparted by One who is Himself living ; and the laws of matter cannot have originated in matter itself ; it needed a living Being to impart life, and a sentient Being to impress on matter its forces and its laws. And therefore we are compelled to believe that this wonderful thing which we call life must have been imparted to man and to the animal world by a First Great Cause, who is the Author and Giver of life, as well as of every other good and perfect gift. Some, I am aware, believe that evolution is consistent with revelation, or at least with the argument from design. For them it may be easy to accept the unproved and, I must say, to me, untenable scientific hypothesis that man has been spontaneously evolved out of the monera ; for me it is much less difficult to receive the account of his origin as stated in Genesis, that " God created man in His own image, in the image of God created He him, male and female created He them." It is pleasant to leave the search after the origin of man in animals of a low simian type, and to come to the Bible story of his creation, and to see him walking with God in the garden of the Lord. Man I believe to be directly God-created, not ape-descended. His origin is sublime, and his destiny glorious ; and I summon the very stones in the temple-walls of Egypt to cry out against a theory which appears incompatible with a belief in the Christian Scriptures, and opposed to the statements of the Christian creeds.

Sir William Dawson, the author of *Modern Science in Bible Lands*, says :—" The speculations as to the derivation of man from lower animals often obtruded by popular writers on a too credulous public, and sometimes even confidently stated as if established results of science, have as yet no basis in archæology or geology, since no transitional form between man and beast has been discovered. Even Haeckel, the great German apostle of the evolution of man, has to admit in his imaginary table of derivation two missing links still unknown to science. That man, with his physical peculiarities and high spiritual endowments, could have originated spontaneously or accidentally from any inferior animal known to us, is simply incredible." If the doctrine of evolution were true, surely man's progress would not have come to a sudden and abrupt pause some three or four thousand years ago ; it would have continued since then, and there would be proofs that his physical and spiritual development had never been interrupted. But though attempts have been made to give a series of the ancestors of man as developed in geological time, the attempts have failed. There are no discoverable links between the highest specimen of the ape and the lowest type of man. There are frequent gaps in the series, and the missing links have not been supplied.

Again, on the theory of evolution, why should physical or mental development ever cease? That it has ceased, or not been uniformly progressive, is evident. Has man, in grandeur of conception or in powers of execution, surpassed the builders of these colossal pyramids, these awe-inspiring sphinxes, these splendid palaces and temples? Are these, the earliest monuments of the race, the work of the descendants of the ape and the baboon? Where is the development now? Are the modern Egyptians, in mental capacity or physical strength, in art or in science, superior to the men who reared the obelisk and hollowed out the tomb? Has not Egypt, the fountain of civilization, which drew an Herodotus, a Euclid, a Strabo, and a Plato to visit her universities, and to learn in her schools, become one of the lowest of the nations, needing the occupation of a foreign power to guard her frontier and to control her finance? If the theory of evolution had in it any truth,—if man had to progress through an age of stone, and bronze, and iron, before he reached civilization, then the earliest nations should be the least developed, and be but little removed from the brute. But Egypt, the oldest historic

nation, refutes this idea ; and her majestic monuments
with their frescoes and sculptures, through which we
read the daily life of the king, the priests, and the
people, prove that in the times nearest to the creation
of man she had attained to a higher condition of
importance and greatness than she has ever attained
since. Hers is a development of degeneration. The
descendants of this wonderful people, in outward
appearance resembling the men we see in the sculptures and bas-reliefs on the monuments, can do nothing like them now, and cannot build or paint or
write as their fathers builded and painted and wrote,
cannot model the colossal statue or raise the magnificent pyramid. They have retrograded rather than
advanced. They have lost the power of doing such
works ; their evolution is from higher to lower.

Let me confirm this opinion by a sentence from
Miss Martineau's *Eastern Life, Past and Present.*
In speaking of the glories of the temple at Karnak,
she says :—" Here was enthroned the human intellect
when humanity was elsewhere scarcely emerging
from chaos. And how was it now? That morning
I had seen the governor of Thebes, crouching on his
haunches on the filthy shore among the dung-heaps,
feeding himself with his fingers, among a circle of
apish creatures like himself."

Nor are the Egyptians the only evidences that man's condition has not always been one of growth : history shows many remarkable and indisputable cases of degradation. The Santhals, a tribe of North-east Bengal, are, as is well known, a case in point.

But this is not all. We learn from pictures in the halls of temples and the chambers of tombs that animals and plants arc the same now as they were some four thousand years ago. The lion and the ass are the same ; the horse and the ox are the same ; the hippopotamus and the giraffe have undergone no change ; the hawk and the pigeon show no variation. No doubt there has been what may be termed an in-direct development of some kind of animals or birds since ; but the production of these varieties is due to the agency of man. The word evolution is made to cover so much that it leads to great mental confusion. But, I would ask, has man, though he can produce cross-breeds, ever been able to develop a living ani-mal from dead matter? Has it ever been a proved fact in science that from the instinct of the brute has been evolved the nobler reason of man ? Nay, we have not only the evidence of the sculptured men and animals, but we have the very men and animals and birds themselves of that age ; for they have been preserved for our inspection by the process of embalming. There are mummies of men and women, mummies of kings and queens and priests ; and there are mummies of birds and beasts. The hawk, a sacred bird, is often seen in this form ; and so is also another sacred bird, now extinct—the beautiful ibis. We meet with mummies of the dog, the crocodile, and the cat. The great naturalist, Cuvier, has examined some of these, and this is his testimony :—" I have endeavoured to collect all the ancient documents respecting the forms of animals, and there are none equal to those furnished by the Egyptians, both in regard to their antiquity and abundance. They have not only left us representations of animals, but even their identical bodies embalmed and preserved in the catacombs. I have examined with the greatest attention the engraved figures of quadrupeds and birds upon the numerous obelisks brought from Egypt to ancient Rome ; and all these figures, one with another, have a perfect resemblance to their intended objects, such as they still are in our days. My learned colleague, M. Geoffrey Saint Hilaire, convinced of the importance of this research, carefully collected in the tombs and temples of Upper and Lower Egypt as many mummies of animals as he could procure. He has brought home the mummies of cats, ibises, birds of prey, dogs, monkeys, crocodiles, and the head of a

bull; and after the most attentive and detailed examination, not the smallest difference is to be perceived between these animals and those of the same
species which we now see, any more than between the
human mummies and the skeletons of men of the
present day. Some slight differences are discoverable
between ibis and ibis, for example, just as we now
find differences in the descriptions of naturalists;
but I have removed all doubts on that subject in a
memoir on the ibis of the ancient Egyptians, in
which I have clearly shown that this bird is precisely
the same in all respects at present that it was in the
days of the Pharaohs. I am aware that in these I
only cite the monuments of two or three thousand
years back, but this is the most remote antiquity to
which we can resort in such a case."

I have stated these facts at length because some
scientific men have so confidently asserted this theory
of causal evolution, that many are induced to accept
it as final, and it is received as if it were a new
gospel; and so they allow themselves to be led away
by assumptions which have never been proved, and
do not admit of proof. The theories of evolution
have never passed into demonstration; and though
some hold a contrary opinion, I cannot help believing
that this creed of a world blindly self-developed, of

the descent of man from the brutes,—or, as it has
been forcibly expressed, "the essential bestiality of
man,"—is absolutely fatal to all religion. Instead of
raising our thoughts to an Almighty, all-wise, and
benevolent Creator, it proclaims as the origin of all
the beautiful and harmonious life of nature, a cold
and inert, unintelligent protoplasm. So far as I can
gather from what I have read, this theory of evolution
has had its day ; there are signs that a reaction has
already begun, and that it will ultimately be discarded
even by those who too hastily adopted it as a truth.
And well that it is so, the sooner this gross material-
ism, which ignores a Divine creative will, perishes,
the better. For the presence and condition of man
in the world cannot be satisfactorily accounted for
either by evolution or natural selection,—can only be
accounted for by the belief in his descent from a pair
who were made perfect at first by the fiat of a beneficent and Almighty Being. I know that this faith
is considered folly by Professor Haëckel, who says :—
"It is much more to my individual taste to be the
more highly developed descendant of a primal ape,
who in the struggle for existence had developed pro-
gressively from lower mammals, as they from still
lower vertebrates, than the degraded descendant of an
Adam, God-like, but debased by the fall." Well, *de*

gustibus nil disputandum,—there is no accounting for tastes ; but besides this, the Professor here takes no account of man's spiritual powers,—takes no notice at all of that higher nature by which he is related to God. Which is the more important part of man,—his bodily organism, by which he is related to the beasts below him, or his spiritual nature, by which he is related to God above him ? The truth that man was made in the image of God is the only rational basis of revelation ; for if there were not something within us akin to God, how could we form any conception of God,—of His holiness or justice, His Fatherhood or love ? We could have no idea of God at all, unless we had been made in His image. What can a beast know of God ? What can a beast know even of man ?

Here, too, we see how natural is the Incarnation ; for what more natural than that the Eternal Son should take the form of man, seeing that man was made in the likeness of God? Here, moreover, we see how easy of acceptance becomes the doctrine of man's renewal by the Spirit. " God breathed into man's nostrils the breath of life, and he became a living soul ; " and now for his restoration from the death of sin to the life of righteousness he receives the inspiration of the Almighty,—the inbreathing of the Spirit of God.

And once more I see in this truth of man's being moulded by God in His image how natural are those glorious hopes that shine like a flood of light on our path through the world. If man had only a lower nature,—if he sprang from a primordial germ, enveloped in a mass of protoplasm, and only through a long line of simial and other beasts arrived at his present condition,—how could we believe the glorious things spoken in the Bible of his destiny? If we were only beasts in descent, we could not rise to these conceptions of our future greatness. If we are bestial in descent, why then we may die and rot like the beasts, and it may be that Tyndall is right : "That our end shall be in accordance with our beginning, and that at last our destiny and highest hope shall be, to melt into the infinite azure of the past." But when we think of ourselves as made in the image of God, and that for us God became man, and that in us the Spirit may dwell, it does not seem unreasonable or extravagant that we should share in the glory of God.

I hope these thoughts may be forgiven in a book of travel. They have been pressed upon me by what I saw in Egypt, and learnt of its philosophy, its science, its religion, and its art. I believe that Egypt is a witness to the truth of God in more ways than one, and has been closely connected in the past with sacred history, and with God's dealings with men.

I believe, too, there are blessings in store for this land. Egypt once preserved the Church from death by famine, and gave a Lawgiver to Israel and the world. Egypt gave an asylum to the holy family, when the life of the infant Saviour was threatened by Herod. The gospel found an early entrance into this country; and St. Mark was sent by St. Peter to Alexandria to plant a Christian Church, and the evangelist in time became bishop of the city, and died a martyr's death. St. Athanasius formulated in Alexandria the theology of the Church; and his statement of Christian doctrine was for a time universally accepted as the creed of Christendom. To Egypt we are indebted for the first translation of the Hebrew Scriptures into the Greek language. We owe a great debt of gratitude to this land; and God, who has used it for the propagation of His truth, is not forgetful of its work of faith and labour of love; and He who repays even the cup of cold water given to a disciple in His name, will not be unmindful of the aid which it has rendered to His people and Himself.

And so we find many promises to Egypt in Scripture. And as the words of the prophets, which pre-

dicted her fall, have been fully accomplished, so shall
the prophecies of her rise be faithfully fulfilled. How
literally has the prediction of Jeremiah been accomplished, that Nebuchadrezzar should break the pillars
of Beth-shemesh, the Egyptian On, or Heliopolis ;
and burn the temples of the gods of the Egyptians,
using the element which they worshipped for the
destruction of the shrine where the sun-god was
adored. "I will kindle a fire in the houses of the
gods of Egypt ; and he shall burn them, and carry
them away captives : and he shall array himself with
the land of Egypt, as a shepherd putteth on his garment ; and he shall go forth from thence in peace.
He shall break also the images of Beth-shemesh (the
house of the sun), that is in the land of Egypt ; and
the houses of the gods of the Egyptians shall he
burn with fire" (Jer. xliii. 12, 13). The City of the
Sun is a ruin ; her temple is destroyed ; its university
is gone ; and the solitary obelisk still pointing to the
skies is all that marks the place which was once the
seat of learning, the centre of Egyptian religion, where
kings reigned, and priests ministered at their splendid
shrines.

Now look at the promises to this country. One
will be sufficient for quotation. "In that day shall
there be an altar to the Lord in the midst of the land

of Egypt, and a pillar at the border thereof. And it shall be for a sign and for a witness unto the Lord of hosts in the land of Egypt : for they shall cry unto the Lord because of the oppressors, and He shall send them a Saviour, and a great one, and He shall deliver them. And the Lord shall be known to Egypt, and the Egyptians shall know the Lord in that day, and shall do sacrifice and oblation ; yea, they shall vow a vow unto the Lord, and perform it. And the Lord shall smite Egypt : He shall smite and heal it : and they shall return even to the Lord, and He shall be entreated of them, and shall heal them. In that day shall there be a highway out of Egypt to Assyria, and the Assyrian shall come into Egypt, and the Egyptian into Assyria, and the Egyptians shall serve with the Assyrians. In that day shall Israel be the third with Egypt and with Assyria, even a blessing in the midst of the land : whom the Lord of hosts shall bless, saying, Blessed be Egypt My people, and Assyria the work of My hands, and Israel Mine inheritance " (Isa. xix. 19-25).

As Egypt was given over to idolatry, and raised her temples to false gods, so shall she raise temples to the one true God, and establish worship in His name, and offer the pure sacrifices of prayer and praise, and obedience to His will ; and as the people were smitten for their sins, so they shall be healed on their conversion, and shall live in peace with their great enemy, the Assyrians, and there shall be inter-communion between the two nations, and both shall be the servants of God. Restored Israel, a third people with Egypt and Assyria, shall with them be "a blessing in the midst of the land." Our own days have witnessed the formation of a highway from Egypt into Assyria by the establishment of the new route to India ; through the Suez Canal, ships continually pass to the Persian Gulf and the Euphrates. God works by means, and overrules the necessities of commerce and of politics for the fulfilment of His will. Through His providence, England has now much in her power. By wise and firm counsels, by just administration and right example, she may use her great influence for the promotion of the temporal, moral, and spiritual welfare of the country, and raise it in the scale of nations, may—in this land so long misgoverned and oppressed—bring it, under God, to pass that (if I may with all reverence apply the words), " Truth shall spring out of the earth, and righteousness look down from heaven. Mercy and truth shall meet together ; righteousness and peace shall kiss each other."

It was with regret that I left Cairo, with its

picturesque streets, its grand mosques, and Oriental bazaars, its pleasant drives, and the ever-varying kaleidoscope of colour which is always a delight to the eye. I was sorry, too, to leave the many friends who added so much, by their kindness, to the enjoyment of our stay in the great city. Sorry, too, I was to bid farewell to Egypt, with its massive monuments and majestic temples, its ancient tombs and colossal statues ; the glory of its sunsets, the splendour of its after-glows ; its stately palms, and the changing light on river and desert and plain. It is all like a dream now, but not a dream which one awakes only to forget, but a dream which, like " a thing of beauty, is a joy for ever," and has enriched the memory for all the coming years.

APPENDIX.

I AM indebted to Thomas D. Saville, M.D., M.R.C.P., whose acquaintance I had the pleasure of making in Egypt, for the following observations on the climate on the Nile during the months of winter. They may be of interest to those who intend to spend the winter in that most interesting and delightful country.

Egypt has longer periods of fine weather than almost any winter climate. A high and steady barometer is generally supposed to be indicative of fine weather. But by readings in January, February, and March, on only six occasions did it reach or exceed 30 inches, and it only once reached 30·15. The explanation of this is the remarkable dryness of the air.

In January, the highest maximum temperature was 77°, the lowest minimum 40° (two readings during the night); the average maximum 70·3°, the average minimum 47·2. The average temperature of the month 60°. (Note.—All temperature readings are on the Fahrenheit scale. They were always made in the shade, and the two instruments were fully exposed to the air.) On four days in this month, January, there were slight showers, between Kalabsheh and Aboo Simbel, but they seem to have been local ; eight other days partially cloudy ; fifteen bright and sunny all day. Light and fresh northerly breezes were the prevailing winds. The average fall after sundown of six readings was 3°. Forty observations were made during this month on the humidity of the atmosphere, by means of the wet and dry bulb method, and the percentage (saturation being represented by 100) calculated by Glaisher's Hygrometrical tables. The highest record of the month was 88 per cent., on January 21st, at Aboo Simbel ; and five times it exceeded 80. The lowest of the month was 34 per cent., at Assouan ; and there were eighteen readings below 60. The average percentage of the month of January was 62.

Between February 1st and March 11th the highest maximum temperature at Assouan was 100 ; there were six readings of 90 and upwards. The lowest minimum during the period was 44°, at Assiout. Here were nine readings below 50. The average maximum was 84·5° ; the average minimum was 54·2° ; and the average daily temperature between these dates was

67·7°. There were two showers, each of a few minutes' duration, at Luxor in February; but between February 1st and March 11th there were only six days which were more or less cloudy; the remaining thirty-three were bright and sunny. The prevailing winds were northerly—fresh during February, and stormy during March. There were two days of moderate khamseen, or desert wind, in February, and two in the early part of March. The average fall at sundown was 3·8°. In February and the early part of March the highest recorded percentage humidity was 80° (at Ayat, just above Cairo); but there were four times when the percentage was about 60. The lowest recorded was 24, but there were thirteen occasions when it went below 40. The average percentage humidity during that period, when fifty-three observations were made at all hours of the day, was 49·5°. During the three months I spent in Egypt, there were only three showery days, and only three others on which a few drops of rain fell, not amounting to a shower. At Luxor, no shower had fallen since July 11th, 1887. There were upwards of sixty-five days in three months when the sun was not obscured by cloud. The mean temperature for this space of time was 65·1 Fahr., which corresponds approximately to the July and August average in and near London.

It might be thought that on or near a river so broad and shallow as the Nile, and with its sloping mud banks, the climate would be damp; but facts show the contrary. Humidity recorded on the Nile gives an average of 53·3 per cent. (saturation being represented by 100) between January 1st and March 11th, as compared with an average of 91 per cent. in London at the same time of year, and 76 per cent. in July and August, the driest months in England.

Therefore, as regards quantity of sun, small rainfall, and dryness of atmosphere, winter on the Nile will bear very favourable comparison with any winter climate with which I am acquainted.

Another advantage in winter is the bracing character of the air. The prevailing wind is from the north, blowing from the sea 500 or 1,000 miles away, and coming across the desert; and even in the east and west winds there are bracing properties hardly to be expected in so warm a climate. Another advantage: though there is a fall of temperature at night, there is no dew; because, perhaps, the rapid radiation and cooling down of the earth's surface is unable to reduce the adjacent atmosphere to cooling point. Even when the air contains 88 per cent. of moisture, there is no dew.

The nights are often cold, as low as 40°. The
average diurnal range for the three months was
28·5°, but it was often much more than this. On
thirteen occasions it amounted to 30° and upwards; on six occasions to 35° and upwards; and
once to 43°.

The coldest time in the twenty-four hours is always
at night, between three and four o'clock in the morning. It is unsafe for invalids and delicate people to
have their windows open all night.

The khamseen blows from the south or south-west,
and scorches like the blast of a furnace, and brings
with it clouds of fine dust and sand. Guide-books
say it rarely comes on till April ; but it often begins
in February, usually in March (as this year), and lasts
fifty days, as its name implies. It blows at intervals,
there being cooler days between. Residents say that
May and June are delightful. The most equable and
delicious climate is at Luxor. Assouan is intolerably
hot, hotter than Wady Halfa, 200 miles farther .
south, and within the tropics ; no doubt because of
the hills which surround Assouan on all sides. The
Nile water should be boiled and filtered, otherwise
there is a risk of diarrhœa and zymotic disease.

The following particulars have been kindly furnished
by the Meteorological Office :—

M.O., 1757.

METEOROLOGICAL OFFICE,

September 18*th*, 1888.

THE AVERAGE MONTHLY RAINFALL AND
RELATIVE HUMIDITY AT LONDON.

Month.	Rainfall in inches.	Rel. Humidity (Saturation = 100).
January	2·20	91
February	1·89	91
March	1·43	86
July	2·17	76
August	2·20	79

NOTE.—The values of Rainfall given above are
based on the observations for twenty years, 1866-1885.
The values of the Relative Humidity are based on
fifteen years' observations (*taken at* 8 *a.m. each day*),
1871-1885.

For the purposes of comparison the values of the
Relative Humidity at the *Kew Observatory* are ap-
pended.   These are based on ten years' *hourly
readings*, 1878–1887.

Kew, Rel. Humidity.

January	. . . 85·9%.
February	. . . 85·3.
March	. . . 77·5.
July	. . . 72·1.
August	. . . 74·5.